THE POOR OF YAHWEH

THE POOR OF YAHWEH

by

Rev. Albert Gelin, P.S.S.

translated by Mother Kathryn Sullivan, R.S.C.J.

THE LITURGICAL PRESS,
Collegeville, Minnesota

Also available:

THE PSALMS ARE OUR PRAYERS

by

Rev. Albert Gelin, P.S.S.

The Poor of Yahweh is the authorized English translation of *Les Pauvres de Yahvé*, third revised edition, by Albert Gelin, P.S.S., published by Les Éditions du Cerf, Paris, France.

Nihil obstat: John Eidenschink, O.S.B., J.C.D., *Censor deputatus.* *Imprimatur:* ✠ Peter W. Bartholome, D.D., Bishop of St. Cloud. August 21, 1963.

Foreword

Once more the English-speaking world is deeply indebted to Mother Kathryn Sullivan, R.S.C.J., for the careful and fluent translation of a work which deserves to be read in every language of the globe. Her labor of love has made it possible for an eminent author to continue speaking, even though death has stilled his voice forever.

His was a voice which time must not silence. A scholar of the first rank, Father Gelin possessed more than scientific erudition. Like the biblical wise man he was a craftsman in the word of God, touching each theme he handled with deep reverence and glowing faith. Some might say that he died prematurely, for he was only fifty-one. But during the short span of his active life he had accomplished much. From a rich mind stored with the science of the Scriptures and from a full heart warmed with devotion to God's word, he illumined the world of scholarship and the lives of men with countless articles and books. His was that gift of holy wisdom which St. Thomas celebrates as an endowment of both mind and heart, "the knowledge which breathes love" (*Summa* I, Q. 43, *Art.* 5).

No better encomium of him can be written than the words with which the grandson of Jesus ben Sirach celebrated the memory of his grandfather:

> Those who are familiar with these truths must not only understand them themselves but, as lovers of wisdom, be able, in speech and in writing, to help others less familiar. Such a one was my grandfather, Jesus, who, having de-

> voted himself for a long time to the diligent study of the Law, the Prophets, and the rest of the books of our ancestors, and having developed a thorough familiarity with them, was moved to write something himself in the nature of instruction and wisdom, in order that those who love wisdom might, by acquainting themselves with what he had written, make even greater progress in living in conformity with the divine law (*foreword to the Book of Sirach*).

Of all that Father Gelin wrote, *The Poor of Yahweh* will probably live longest in the minds of men. He here develops a theme which looms large in modern study of the spirit of the Bible. He treats of the *'anawim*, "the poor and needy," who rise out of the pages of the Old Testament as the true people of God. The pattern of their holiness forms the blueprint for the Scriptural portrayal of the great saints of Israel: Moses, Samuel, Jeremiah, Anna and Judith. The voice of the *'anawim* is resonant in the prayerful pleading of the songs of the Psalter. Their spirit fills the souls of the holy ones in the New Testament: Joseph and Mary, Zachary and Elizabeth. In the Matthean form of the Beatitudes, the *'anawim* model of holiness is described and codified as the ideal Christian character.

In writing the present work Father Gelin drew abundantly from previous studies on "the poor of Israel." His wide research in the relevant literature enriched his insights, centering his attention on elements of Scriptural revelation which otherwise he might have missed. Some scholars, however, are of the opinion that his extensive reading of works about the Bible obscured his perspective and brought him to conclusions which are not warranted by the biblical text itself. They seriously question whether Father Gelin and the scholars of his school can find in the Scriptural *donnée* a sound basis for their thesis that "poverty of spirit" forms the leit-motiv of Israel's response to God. After a painstaking analysis of the vocabulary of poverty in the Old Testament, these critics have concluded that literature on the *'anawim* has created a character which has no proportionate counterpart in the pages of the Bible.

Those who object to Father Gelin's treatment have offered a careful study in biblical semantics to support their criticism. But they have overlooked the fact that vocabulary analysis is never a final determinant of the content of Scriptural themes. All the elements of biblical teaching, all the features of character portrayal, all the prayers of Israel must be taken into account if one is to reach a total view of a doctrine or spirit which the Old Testament inculcates.

This is the task which Father Gelin has accomplished, an analysis for which his own special gift of wisdom equipped him. Certain texts which he cites may be too fragile to support the generalizations which he rests on them. A reading of his book, however, will show that his conclusions repose solidly on the foundations of the whole expanse of Scriptural teaching.

The parallels which he draws from the liturgy and the sanctity of the modern Church show that he has pursued his investigation under the light of the analogy of faith. With keen awareness of what is univocal in the grace of the Old and New Testaments, he has traced revealing likenesses which illumine the pages of Scripture. His delicate blending of the ancient and the contemporary gives living warmth to an age-old theme and renders it vitally practical in the lives of men today. Like the truly wise householder, he brings out "old things and new."

The appearance of his work in an English translation is especially timely in this period of the Church's Pentecostal renewal through the Spirit-guided action of the Second Vatican Council. The Bishops of the world have often spoken of poverty in eloquent discourses on the floor of the Council. They have described the crying needs of their people in underprivileged countries. They have emphasized the urgency for clergy and laity alike to show forth in deeds the spirit of detachment and unselfishness which Christ asked of His followers. They have underscored the truth that, to reach the vast majority of men, the Church of Christ must be the Church of the poor. The message of our Bishops will be lost upon many if the poverty of spirit recommended by the Council is seen only as material destitution. God has never put His blessing on merely physical misery. Through the prophets and apostles, through the messianic mercy of His own Son, He worked always to save men from the blight of hunger, nakedness and disease.

What He really wants is poverty of spirit, the denial of covetous desire and the charity of self-giving, which alone open the heart to perfect love of God and to generous love of men. The burdens of merely material poverty can crush the soul's aspirations and torture the mind with dark, hidden cravings to be satisfied at any price. This is not poverty of spirit. Only when the poor see in their misery an external sign of their complete dependence upon God, only when the well-to-do are free of clutching possessiveness, only when all men hold their hearts open to God and their hands widespread to their neighbor, only then are the sons of God truly poor in spirit, like the *'anawim* of the Scriptures whose eyes are always turned to the Lord and whose ears are always alert to the cry of the needy. It is in this sense that the Church of Christ must be today, as it was in the beginning, the Church of the *'anawim*.

One suggestive thought Father Gelin has left unsaid, though it breathes throughout the whole spirit of his book. Had he given expression to this word, it would have crowned all that he has written so beautifully on the "poor of Yahweh." Speaking of Christ, St. Paul writes: "He learned obedience through the things which He suffered" (Heb. 5:8). The Greek word here used for "obedience" (*hypakouē*) is often used in the Septuagint translation of the Old Testament to render the Hebrew word for "poverty" (*'anawah*). Like ourselves, therefore, the Son of God too had to learn "poverty of spirit." In living and dying as man He became the greatest of the *'anawim*, our perfect model in following that spirit which Father Gelin here describes so well and which Mother Sullivan brings to us with the crystalline clarity of her translation.

Barnabas M. Ahern, C.P.
Passionist Fathers Seminary
Louisville, Kentucky

Contents

Introduction

The problem of the "poor of Yahweh" has attracted biblical scholars since Graetz (1882-1883). Twice since then, interest has been sharply focused on these fervent souls. During the first period the ideas of Graetz and Loeb (1890-1892) were clarified, corrected and developed. Rahlfs' study (1892) was accepted as normative. Later came Causse's brilliant and suggestive work (1922). It is not without significance that in the Gunkel-Begrich translation of the psalms (1933) the poor of Yahweh are given a place which seems theirs by right.

In 1939 the question was re-examined in the climate of thought characteristic of the biblical revival. Men were looking for a spirituality that would be warm, concrete, vital. Their need led them to study the interior life of the Old Testament men whom they so closely resembled. At the same time other thinkers — existentialists like Karl Jaspers, for example — opened men's minds to the dialectic of failure and the conditions of the wager of faith. The modern "biblical man" found these ideas congenial. Were they not the product of troubled times, similar to those in which the *'anawim* were fashioned?

The portrait sketched here of God's clients amply illustrates their sense of community, their faith and their hope, giving us the perfect *type* of the biblical man in a frame of reference at once historical and psychological. The biblical man is the man who remains in God's presence: "The Lord before whose face I stand" (3 Kings 18:15). The poor of Yahweh lived in God's presence, totally committed, fully surrendered, blindly confident. Jeremiah, it will be remembered, had an essential place in this mystic lineage, and the present study (the second of a trilogy) will have more to say about him and his disciples. With the Virgin of the *Magnificat,* the line reached its summit; with Jesus it reached its perfection.

"The more you are poor, the more Jesus will love you." This thought of St. Thérèse of the Child Jesus better expresses our purpose than do pages of learned lexicons. The "poverty" to which it refers is a spiritual experience, as simple as the "faith" of St. Paul. Those who live this simplicity understand it. Yet, to try to grasp its secret, it must be situated in relation to real poverty (which is its fertile soil), in relation to humility (which is its soul), in relation to faith (of which it is a modality).

Earlier works have made this analysis possible. Yet this little book is more than a summary. May its suggestions as well as its mistakes draw attention to an important biblical development.

In different parts of the world powerful vibrations have been noted to an experience of spiritual poverty. Moslem scribes copy their sacred texts, then add in the colophon after their name, *al faqîr lillâh,* "the poor of Allah." Hindu *baktis,* who know what it is to be poor, are more open to Christianity than yogis who claim to enjoy heavenly visions through their own power. It exorcises the old pharisaical spirit which is the biblical term for our pelagianisms and our laicisms. "Modern man," according to Brunschvicq, "needs no redemption."

I end this little book in the village where my master and friend, Father Chaine, spent his last years. His biblical teaching had all the beauty of the source whence he drew his inspiration because his life was a true commentary on the Beatitudes. I like to think that his friends, when reading these pages, will think of him.

Albert Gelin, P.S.S.
Saint-Vincent de Reins
France

THE POOR OF YAHWEH

CHAPTER 1

Old Testament Thoughts about Poverty

There are many references in the Old Testament to poverty as a social phenomenon. No other ancient literature contains such detailed descriptions, nor so considered a judgment. Poverty was obviously something that shocked thoughtful Israelites. Yet it is difficult to reconcile the reactions which they expressed at different times in different ways. Is the explanation to be found in the intellectual temperament of these biblical authors who were less concerned than we are about logical consistency and more accustomed to successive descriptions of the complex aspects of reality? May it not also be due to the fact that these voices were raised in many different circumstances?

An examination of the texts suggests that there were three lines of thought. The first, and the most important, considered poverty as a scandalous condition that should never have existed in Israel. The origin of this line of thought is found in the religion of Moses. When he established the people of God in the deserts of Sinai and Kadesh, he gave them a common soul and a kind of collectivist sensibility, facilitated by the seminomadic structure of their life. As a result of this quasi-organic solidarity, individuals lived and acted as a function of the whole; the individual was to the group what the member was to the living body.[1] Hopes, trials, pos-

[1] See A. Causse, *Du groupe ethnique à la communauté religieuse* (Paris: 1937), pp. 21ff.

sessions, all were shared. The blessings foreseen and promised by Yahweh were to be enjoyed by all. Later the Deuteronomist, who was to create the myth of the desert in his effort to remodel Israel according to the original plan, evoked the ideal of a brotherhood where there was no poverty.

The fate of this ideal, when the Israelites became sedentary in Canaan, is well known. They had to adapt themselves to the conditions of a peasant civilization which left little room for individual projects or initiative. Chance or mischance interfered. The quality of the soil, the frequency of raids, intermarriage with indigent natives who clung jealously to ancient agricultural customs, were so many factors of success or failure. Larger landholdings became the great objective: the desire to increase their acreage, in ways that do not bear scrutiny, contradicted the terms of the tenth commandment as formulated by Moses (Ex. 20:17; cf. Micah 2:2).

No doubt the regular reunion of the Israelite amphictyony[2] recalled past norms and the sacral act of the seventh year, which made the products of the soil available to all and gave Hebrew slaves their freedom (Ex. 21:2ff; 23:10-11), thus renewing Israel's primitive unity. The efficacy of this "going back to the beginning" cannot be overestimated; it corrected history's course and peasants' calculations.

The rise of urban civilization coincided with the ascendancy of royal civilization and only aggravated this evil. In towns, guilds of workers were formed in which membership was restricted to skilled craftsmen; this destroyed traditional social structures. To the towns came wealthy landowners who took advantage of depressions and wars to round out their domains and introduce a system of latifundia (Is. 5:8) which separated them from the rural proletariat they were creating. The kings, in whom the people were unified and through whom they were "blessed," took part in this movement instead of controlling it.

[2] The word *amphictyony* was introduced by Noth and has become part of exegetical literature. It denotes a federation of tribes centered about a common sanctuary, e.g., Kadesh under Moses, Schechem under Joshua.

As early as the reign of David signs of social dislocation could be discerned: David made himself dependent on a guard recruited in foreign lands, encouraged an amalgam of Israelite and non-Israelite, superimposed an administrative corps of men without family background or political experience upon old, traditional social patterns. The regal splendor of the palace, the burden of taxes, international involvements (trade, war and treaties) introduced a new "climate." The Bible's first anti-royalist diatribe is with good reason pronounced by Samuel at the birth of the monarchy; it was a defense of the average man who, even in Solomon's lifetime, paid the price of royal luxury and prestige (1 Sam. 8:10-18).[3]

The prophets were the conscience of Israel and they worked to preserve the Mosaic heritage. We call them revolutionaries because of their violent attacks against the established order. Admittedly, they did speak in the name of the past, but they were not blindly conservative.[4] They had gone back to ancient days to find the essential inspiration of the religious ideal they wished to restore in a firmly established society. Deeply-rooted loyalty to tradition was their characteristic.

When a return to this tradition became possible, the prophets were ready: Ahijah of Shiloh stood beside Jeroboam when he rose against Solomon; Elisha supported Jehu when he set out to destroy the house of Ahab. Elijah, Elisha's master, defended Naboth's inheritance against the king himself, and he was but the thundering echo of a tradition that respected the rights of every member of the Israelite alliance.

Because the great prophets championed the weak, they never stopped denouncing oppression in every form: fraudulent transactions (Hosea 12:8; Amos 8:5), large landholdings

[3] As a background for this paragraph, see J. Pedersen, *Israel, Its Life and Culture* (London: 1940), III-IV, 63ff.

[4] Some authors are inclined to stress the anti-Canaan and anti-civilization aspects of the prophets' reactions. For example, P. Humbert, "Osée, le prophète bédouin," *Revue d'Histoire et de Philosophie Religieuses*, I, 97-118; A. Causse, *Les pauvres d'Israël* (Paris: 1922), pp. 53ff. But the prophet accepted an agrarian civilization, and Isaiah 28:23-29 looked on agriculture as an art taught by God. According to other writers, Isaiah expressed his messianism in terms of a royal civilization.

(Micah 2:1-3; Ezek. 22:29), venal judges (Amos 5:7), enforced slavery (Neh. 5:1-5),[5] the violence of the proprietary class — the *'am ha'areṣ*[6] — and heartless officials, among whom must be included the kings themselves (Jer. 22:13-17):

> ...you that turn judgment into wormwood and forsake justice in the land! (Amos 5:7).

> They are grown gross and fat, and have most wickedly transgressed my words. They have not judged the cause of the widow, they have not managed the cause of the fatherless, and they have not judged the judgment of the poor (Jer. 5:28).

Similar protestations, from Amos to Zechariah, are easily found. It is important to grasp their true meaning. The prophets did not romanticize the poor: Jeremiah was willing to attack the quality of the faith of both poor and rich (Jer. 5:4); and Isaiah, for the same reasons, delivered both classes to Yahweh's wrath (Is. 9:12-16). The prophets used religious criteria in forming their judgments: rich and poor alike were evaluated in relation to Yahweh and His will. But wealth was soon seen to be a ramp leading to pride and self-sufficiency:

> And Ephraim said: But yet I am become rich, I have found me an idol (Hosea 12:9);

and a slope fatal to lasting social bonds:

> By which her rich men were filled with iniquity, and the inhabitants thereof have spoken lies; and their tongue was deceitful in their mouth. And I therefore began to strike you with desolation for your sins (Micah 6:12-13).

Gladly prophets contrasted the poor man with the sinner (*rašaʻ*). We shall see that Amos compared the poor man with the just man (*ṣaddiq*). According to Mowinckel's perceptive

[5] Nehemiah was influenced largely by the prophets and the Deuteronomist.

[6] The expression, "the people of the land," denotes first of all the landowning classes, proprietors (2 Kings 23:30, 35), as opposed to those who held no land *(dallat ha'areṣ)*. After the exile, the term became a religious one and was used to describe the common man who took no pains to observe the Law and was obstinate in his "impurity."

remark, the poor man is a "just" man in relation to an oppressor who has treated him unjustly and deprived him of primordial rights to covenant blessings that had been guaranteed him by the Sinai pact; the term included the right of appeal (*Rechtsanspruch*).[7] This does not mean that the poor as poor were pleasing to Yahweh, but that God looked on the mistreatment of the poor as an affront to His sovereignty over Israel. He declared in an indictment of the great men of Israel:

> For you have devoured the vineyard,[8] and the spoil of the poor is in your house. Why do you consume my people and grind the faces of the poor? (Is. 3:14-15).

Does not the vocabulary that draws together Yahweh and the poor of Israel show the direction of the Lord's preferences?

In Amos, Yahweh protests:

> ...because he has sold the just man (*ṣaddiq*) for silver and the poor man (*'ebyon*) for a pair of shoes. They bruise the heads of the poor (*dallim*) upon the dust of the earth and turn aside the way of the humble (*'anawim*)—Amos 2:6-7.

Note the terms used. To designate the poor man, the Hebrew has a neutral word, *raš*, which is frequently found in the book of Proverbs. But prophetic preaching and its Deuteronomic extension expressed pity in almost photographic terms. "Poverty was never something to which prophets could be indifferent. When they spoke of it, they protested against the oppression and injustice of the rich and the mighty. Naturally, they found expressions consonant with their feelings."[9]

Père Humbert[10] has made a study of the word *'ebyon*. He derived it from the Hebrew root found also in Akkadian and Ancient Egyptian, *'aba*, to wish, to desire. The *'ebyon* is the

[7] A. Kuschke, "Arm und reich im Alten Testament," *Zeitschrift für die Alttestamentliche Wissenschaft*, 1939, p. 50. See S. Mowinckel, *Awän und die individuellen Klagepsalmen* (1921), pp. 115, 117.

[8] "Vineyard" denotes the "spouse" of Yahweh, the people of Israel.

[9] Van der Ploeg, "Les pauvres d'Israël et leur piété," *Oudtestamentische Studiën*, VII (1950), 258.

[10] "Le mot biblique *'ebyon*," *Rev. d'Hist. et de Phil. Relig.*, 1952, pp. 1-6.

"covetous man", "the poor man considered as seeking, begging. The word indicates not only a need, but also an expectation and a request." An analysis of the context suggests a beggar imploring charity. It occurs for the first time in Exodus 23:6-11, a text that probably belongs to the ninth century. Perhaps it is a foreign word introduced into Israel when pauperism and its corollary, begging, first appeared.

The word *dal* comes from the Hebrew root *dalal,* meaning "to be thin, weak, sickly." The Akkadian and Arabic words corroborate this. It is used in Pharaoh's dream to describe the seven lean (*dalloth*) kine that succeeded the seven plump ones (Gen. 41:19), and in the stereotyped expression *dallat ha'areṣ,* "the thin ones of the land," i.e., the rural proletariat.[11]

The word *'ani,* the passive *qatil* form, comes from the root *'anah II,* which originally meant "to be stooped, bowed, lowered, overwhelmed." According to Birkeland, the *'ani* is "the man who finds that his powers, strength and worth have declined" as the result of present or permanent suffering (*'oni)* due to economic poverty, sickness, prison or oppression. The same nuance is found in the Spanish word *humilhados.*

The word *'anaw* (used only once in the singular) has the same basic meaning as *'ani.* It acquired religious resonances (humble before God) more easily than did the other words. But in several instances, especially in the expression *'anwe ha'areṣ* (poor country people), it was a synonym for *'ani.*

These are the oldest distinctions in the vocabulary of poverty, as far as they can be discovered. Their semantic development will be traced in the following pages. A rigorously consistent translation is difficult, so a transcription of the original will always be supplied.

A few texts will make it possible to sum up the struggle on behalf of the poor so far described. Some say that today new aspects of poverty have appeared, yet what the Old Testament men of God saw was substantially the same: the underprivileged formed a group who cried to Yahweh about their de-humanization, their lack of family stability, their

[11] See footnote 6. The expression may be found in 2 Kings 24:14; 25:12; Jer. 40:7.

need of a home, their inability to earn a livelihood, their oppression, their discouragement. And the prophets repeated their complaints:

> Hear this word, you fat kine that are in the mountains of Samaria, you that oppress the needy (*dallim*) and crush the poor (*'ebyonim*) — Amos 4:1.

> Woe to them that make wicked laws, and when they write, write injustice: to oppress the poor (*dallim*) in judgment, and do violence to the cause of the humble (*'aniyyeey*) of my people (Is. 10:1-2).

> Defend the lowly and the fatherless; render justice to the afflicted (*'ani*) and the destitute (*raš*). Rescue the lowly (*dal*) and the poor (*'ebyon*); from the hand of the wicked deliver them (Ps. 81:3-4).

Of the Messiah it is said:

> But he shall judge the poor (*'anawim*) with justice, and shall reprove with equity for the meek (*dallim*) of the earth (Is. 11:4).

The Deuteronomist lived in a prophetic milieu, and equated *'ani* with *'ebyon*. His legislation was always parenetic and was meant to paralyze pauperism wherever it existed, even among Levites and transients.[12] The year for the remission of debts and the liberation of Hebrew slaves, the prohibition of interest on loans, the order forbidding the acceptance of a poor man's surety, the quarterly contribution for the unfortunate, the daily payment of a worker's wage — these are the institutions that the Deuteronomist justified and stoutly defended. But his friendly exhortation went much further than these carefully specific recommendations: "The needy (*'ebyonim*) will never be lacking in the land; that is why I command you to open your hand to your poor (*'ani*) and needy (*'ebyon*) kinsman in your country" (Deut. 15:11).

In the Wisdom aphorisms, too, reference is made to the needy of Israel, both before and after the exile:

[12] The *ger* or metic is a foreigner who has made his home in Israel and is becoming naturalized. See Franz Buhl, *La société israélite d'après l'Ancien Testament* (Paris: 1904), pp. 75-82.

> If a king is zealous for the rights of the poor (*dallim*), his throne stands firm forever (Prov. 29:14).
>
> The just man has a care for the rights of the poor (*dallim*); the wicked man has no such concern (Prov. 29:7).
>
> He who has compassion on the poor (*dal*) lends to the Lord (Prov. 19:17).

The spirit of the Deuteronomist is also found in the book of Job. From its pages rise to God the cry of the *'ani* and the *dal* (Job 34:28), and a fresco of somber beauty records the scandal of one who refuses to give up his belief in divine justice:

> The wicked remove landmarks; they steal away herds and pasture them. The asses of orphans they drive away; they take the widow's ox for a pledge. They force the needy off the road; all the poor of the land are driven into hiding. Like wild asses in the desert, these go forth to their task of seeking food; the steppe provides food for the young among them; they harvest at night in the untilled land.
>
> They pass the night naked, without clothing, for they have no covering against the cold; they are drenched with the rain of the mountains, and for want of shelter they cling to the rock. Between the rows they press out the oil; they glean in the vineyard of the wicked. They tread the wine presses, yet suffer thirst, and famished are those who carry the sheaves. From the dust the dying groan, and the souls of the wounded cry out....[13]

These groans were to turn into curses. Something like a sacred awe can be discerned in the passage in which Ben Sirach sums up the traditional biblical teaching about the poor. The cry of the poor, like the blood of Abel, rises to the Lord:

> My son, rob not the poor man of his livelihood; force not the eyes of the needy to turn away. A hungry man grieve not, a needy man anger not; do not exasperate the

[13] Job 24:2-12. "This," writes Larcher, "is the most moving description in the whole Bible of the fate of those unfortunate ones who call upon God's justice."

> downtrodden; delay not to give to the needy. A beggar in distress do not reject; avert not your face from the poor. From the needy turn not your eyes, give no man reason to curse you; for if in the bitterness of his soul he curse you, his Creator will hear his prayer (Sir. 4:1-6).

Poverty could never be considered a normal state, in the light of those lessons taught by the spiritual guides of the Chosen People. An examination of their laws and institutions corroborates this.[14] We see the poor man as a victim whom we must pity, a derelict whom we must save. However, there was another line of thought which, if carried to its logical conclusion, would condemn the poor man as a sinner.

The law of temporal retribution, the gift of non-biblical civilizations, was formulated early in the history of Israel and continued to be professed even when Judaism was near its end. Wealth is one of the clearest proofs that the just man is rewarded in this world; he who fears Yahweh prospers in the land of the living and enjoys long life, security, light, blessing, peace, salvation. At first it was thought that Israel, born in a liberating revolution, molded by trials in the desert, made into a nation by the God of retribution, was called as a people to possess the good things of Yahweh. History gave the lie to this ideal. The poor man was stripped of everything except his fundamental right. Since this was inalienable, men hoped that it would be respected in the messianic era (Is. 11:4; Ps. 71:2; Ps. 36:11). The covenant ideal was never far from men's minds.

Yet the ideal had to be squared with the facts. The success in Canaan of one Israelite or another was in itself ambiguous, but men tended to explain this inequality in terms of the law of retribution. Experience showed that virtue was linked with poverty, wealth with wickedness (Prov. 19:1; 28:6; 19:22). But the sages held that the inverse equation was the normal rule. The stereotyped expression, "born of

[14] Compare the Aristotelian perspective in which society is rigidly divided according to natural vocation and where social categories are considered sacred. Cf. "Le temps du pauvre," *Jeunesse de l'Église*, 9, 1948, pp. 37, 110-111.

poor but honest parents," found in so many lives of the saints, shows the persistence of the old formula. Once, when Job dared to question its validity, his friends accused him of failing in reverence (Job 15:4), that is to say, "destroying religion." When the sages referred to poverty, they liked to use an adjective or neuter noun, *raš*. They did not deal gently with the poor man.

> A little sleep, a little slumber, a little folding of the arms to rest — then will poverty *(reʾš)* come upon you like a highwayman, and want like an armed man (Prov. 6:10-11; 24:34).
>
> The slack hand impoverishes, but the hand of the diligent enriches (Prov. 10:4).
>
> Love not sleep, lest you be reduced to poverty; eyes wide open mean abundant food (Prov. 20:13).
>
> ...the drunkard and the glutton come to poverty, and torpor clothes a man in rags (Prov. 23:21).
>
> He who cultivates his land will have plenty of food, but from idle pursuits a man has his fill of poverty (Prov. 28:19).

The tone does not become religious until Prov. 13:18:

> Poverty *(reʾš)* and shame befall the man who disregards correction, but he who heeds reproof is honored.[15]

This is still more pronounced in the idyllic psalms whose truth was challenged by Job, Qoheleth and the *ʿanawim,* of whom mention is made in Psalms 36, 48 and 72. Whatever the just man does succeeds, according to Psalm 1:3.

> Happy the man who fears the Lord, who greatly delights in his commands. His posterity shall be mighty upon the earth; the upright generation shall be blessed. Wealth and riches shall be in his house; his generosity shall endure forever (Ps. 111:1-3).

This hard and narrow interpretation of the law of retribution, this mobilization of divinity as its guarantee, marked

[15] Correction or instruction (Heb. *musar)* was a term indicating the teaching of the sages.

only one phase of Israelite thought. We shall see how one day such ideas were abandoned. Here let us observe that the confrontation of the poor just man and the wicked rich man presents a problem that must be transcended to be solved, either by waiting for the day of Yahweh (Ps. 36), or for the next world (Ps. 72).

In sapiential circles, a third line of thought appeared. If the wise man dreaded penury (which clashed violently with his ideas of earthly well-being), he also recoiled from any excessive pleasure and comfort, because he considered both states to be equally dangerous: the poor man is easily tempted to be dishonest; the man who has everything is easily tempted to be proud.

> Put falsehood and lying far from me; give me neither poverty nor riches; (provide me only with the food I need;) lest, being full, I deny you, saying, "Who is Yahweh?" Or, being in want, I steal, and profane the name of my God (Prov. 30:8-9).

The ideal is an intermediate state befitting men of virtue. The Old Testament had its own way of telling the fable of the lazy workman and the financier. Obviously, the rich have no monopoly of health, strength and happiness (Sir. 29:22; 30:14-16). This is a good introduction to the page where Proudhon rediscovers a Franciscan theme:

> Poverty is decent. Her garments are not ragged like the cynic's cloak. Her home is clean and comfortable. She changes her linen at least once a week. She is neither pale nor hungry-looking. Like Daniel's companions, she thrives on a meager diet, she has enough to eat and she is happy. Poverty is not luxury: it would not be good for a worker to have everything he wants. Lest he be corrupted he must feel the sting of want.... Poverty is good. We should look on it as the source of our happiness.[16]

The Bible, too, grieves over the rich man who "wanders after mammon" (cf. Sir. 31:8). The hypothesis has been proposed that "Yahweh's fervent followers were largely re-

[16] *La guerre et la paix*, ed. M. Rivière (Paris: 1927), p. 338. Charles Péguy studies this same theme in *De Jean Coste*.

cruited from the middle class." We cannot deny their presence, but we know little about them. Van der Ploeg asks us to make a connection between "the poor" and "the pious."[17] We believe, however, that there is a better explanation than this simple factual one.

It is true that the vocabulary of poverty has been enriched with religious values. Its terms are transposed to a spiritual plane. Words that once denoted a sociological reality came to mean an attitude of soul.

Recall the word "slave" (*'ebed)* that was adopted, modified and welcomed as part of the language of religion. Recall the more simple example of the word "proletariat," which Jacques Prévert stripped of its pejorative associations and used to express the ideal of man's human condition. In much the same way the words *'anawim, 'aniyyim, dallim, 'ebyonim* took their place in the vocabulary of the theology of grace.

The poor man became God's client. Poverty meant the ability to welcome God, an openness to God, a willingness to be used by God, a humility before God. The transition from sociology to religion, from material poverty to poverty of soul will be described in the following pages.

[17] Van der Ploeg, *op. cit.*, p. 270.

CHAPTER 2

The Church of the "Poor" from Zephaniah to the Psalmists

The theology of the covenant is the Bible's center of gravity.[1] Without ever revoking the appeal to all mankind that is found in the great texts about Adam, the universal plan that is always in the background of sacred history, actually in fact to facilitate it, God chose a people to be His witness and mediator. Among all the nations of the earth, Israel is the firstfruit (*rešit* — Jer. 2:3), the first-born (*bekor* — Ex. 4:22), a people of priests (Ex. 19:5-6). Thereafter, God and Israel were to work together; the language used to describe their collaboration is affective in tone, that of the nuptial relationship, for instance (Hosea 2:21-22; Jer. 2:2; 3:1; Ezek. 23; Is. 50:1).

Echoes of this relationship can be found in the last verses of the Bible (Apoc. 21:17).[2] God's salvific activity on behalf of the people He has chosen is described as an act of elective "justice" (*ṣedaqah*). Whether this term is used in the singular (Hosea 2:21; Ps. 35:11; Is. 46:12ff.), or in the plural (Judg. 5:11; 1 Sam. 12:6ff.), it carries with it an idea of power and loyalty within the framework of the covenant. Israel, as it

[1] Eichrodt centered his whole biblical theology around the covenant in his *Theologie des alten Testaments*, 2 vols., 4th ed. (Berlin: 1950).

[2] A. Neher has forcibly restated these ideas in *Amos, Contribution à l'étude du prophétisme* (Paris: 1950).

advances along the road of history, constantly encounters God. "Days of Yahweh" succeed one another; His appearances are either beneficent or awe-inspiring, either a reward or a punishment, depending on Israel's moral conduct.

This punishment, in the first perspective of the covenant, could not fail to be medicinal and educational. However, after the eighth century, sins multiplied and their gravity increased. Infringements of justice scandalized Amos; Isaiah knew well that he lived in the midst of men of unclean lips; Zephaniah rebuked Judah for faults of pride; Jeremiah was forced to the conclusion that a state of sin existed that made conversion almost impossible (Jer. 6:30; 13:23). Israel had to learn to accept the sanctions of vindictive justice! Yet these prophets, despite all their somber predictions, never lost hope in God's plan for the future. In their eyes the remnant theme safeguarded the theology of the covenant.[3]

Henceforth, the task and promises which were once entrusted to the people of Israel as a whole would one day belong to a small and select group of Israelites. Amos and later prophets repeated this on every occasion. The idea of the remnant is central in Isaiah (Is. 4:3; 6:13; 7:3). It is, first of all, eschatological: the Israel of tomorrow will be the remnant. Tomorrow is not far off; God will soon fashion a new people. In fact, beginning with Jeremiah (Jer. 31:31-34) and Ezekiel (Ezek. 34:30-31; 36:26-28), the collective dream was focused on the "new covenant" which would at last embrace a people worthy of God. Disappointment followed disappointment and the dream continued to recede. The Jews returning to Judah after the exile proudly claimed that they were the remnant (Neh. 1:3), but a century and a half later, Zechariah (Zech. 13:8-9) predicted that they needed further purification before they could call themselves the people of God.[4]

[3] Cf. A. Descamps, *Les justes et la justice dans les évangiles et le christianisme primitif, hormis la doctrine proprement paulinienne* (Louvain: 1950).

[4] For a study of the "remnant", see S. Garofalo, *La nozione profetica del "Resto d'Israele"* (Rome: 1942).

It must be remembered that the prophets not only announced but also helped to shape the future. They attracted disciples and formed groups that prefigured the reality that was to come. Thus, when Isaiah realized that the people had rejected him, he devoted all his attention to a band of disciples, just as Christ began the formation of His apostles after His failure in Galilee. In Isaiah 8:16 we see for the first time "a religious society that is distinct from the nation."[5] In this way all the prophets had disciples who preserved and edited their master's oracles; sometimes they were reserved, as in the case of Ezekiel, sometimes enthusiastic, as in the case of the Second-Isaiah. This influence was not always direct — in fact, it might even be posthumous, as in the case of Jeremiah. The result was, nevertheless, the same: gradually a remnant was shaped.

In the seventh century the remnant was given a special name that was to last until the coming of Christ and that made them a people apart. The prophet Zephaniah, writing about 640-630, identified the people of the future as a people of "the poor":

> In that day you shall not be ashamed for all your doings wherein you have transgressed against me; for then I will take away out of the midst of you your proud boasters and you shall no more be lifted up because of my holy mountain. And I will leave in the midst of you a poor and needy people; and they shall hope in the name of Yahweh. The remnant of Israel shall not do iniquity nor speak lies, nor shall a deceitful tongue be found in their mouth; for they shall feed and shall lie down, and there shall be none to make them afraid (Zeph. 3:11-13).

Zephaniah witnessed Judah's first great humiliation. At the end of the eighth century Assyria cut the Promised Land in half as the result of Sennacherib's victorious conquest. Jerusalem was saved by a miracle, but Asshur's protective custody left the people little freedom. Perhaps it was this humbling situation that inspired the prophet to choose the suggestive vocabulary in which he formulated his spiritual

[5] Buchanan Gray.

synthesis. Israel's endemic poverty had attracted the charitable pity of the Deuteronomist and the prophets. Amos had sympathized with the stooped (*'ani, 'anaw*) and emaciated man (*dal*). Zephaniah borrowed these words and transfigured them: they ceased to denote failure and became a claim for protection. Man must be poor before God, just as he was already poor in the presence of Asshur. Specifically, this meant the rooting out of all pride. Isaiah had taught the prophet that the essence of sin is excess (Is. 2:6ff). Therefore he invited his contemporaries to spiritual "poverty," which is faith plus abandonment, humility and absolute confidence.

> Seek Yahweh, all you meek (*'anawim*) of the earth, you that have wrought his judgment: seek the just, seek the meek (*'anawah*): if by any means you may be hid in the day of Yahweh's indignation (Zeph. 2:3).

The prophet was addressing a group of fervent souls whom he wished to make more fervent.[6] The word he selected is very much like the word *muslim (musulman:* one who is wholly subject to God). The vocabulary of poverty is directly related to that of justice (*ṣedeq*), because in the Old Testament, religion is most often represented as a system of rights and duties.

The oracle of Zephaniah (3:11-13) announced the future realization of an ideal which he could see taking place before his eyes and which he had helped to realize. He insisted that poverty be substituted for pride and made it the authentic spiritual attitude (3:11). This fundamental position includes the rectitude of the whole moral life (3:13). Lastly, the cove-

[6] There is no reason to consider verse 3 as the marginal gloss of a pious postexilic reader (K. Elliger, *Das Buch der zwölf kleinen Propheten* [Göttingen: 1950], II, 65). Elliger has most successfully established a spiritual synthesis of Zephaniah (cf. *ibid.*, pp. 75-76). Earlier Birkeland (*'ani und 'anaw in den Psalmen*, Oslo, 1933, p. 90) had noted when he referred to Zephaniah as an *epigonus* that "All human haughtiness is sin and pride. But Isaiah did not draw the conclusion and used the term *'ani* to describe man's ideal situation before God. The term *'ani* was chosen to express the ideal relation of man to Yahweh, only by the *epigoni*, prophets who were directly influenced by Isaiah, like Zephaniah in 3:12, where the ideal people of the future is called *'am 'ani wadal.*"

nant vocabulary clarified the vocabulary of poverty and justice: the "remnant" is the "people" of the future, to whom belong the messianic promises of security and abundance (3:12-13). In this statement we find reason to reject the claim of certain exegetes who would attach only a sociological value to the vocabulary of poverty because the messianic people were not to be indigent.[7]

Though few, the oracles of Zephaniah show us that he is a religious genius whose synthesis marks a turning-point in history.

The results of the catastrophe of 587 were utterly unlike those of the Assyrian captivity. Judah's élite was carried into exile, far from familiar securities and structures. But this defeat marked the beginning of a spiritual rebirth whose dimensions Zephaniah can help us to understand.

Political Israel lay in ruins, but a finer Israel was to take its place. Three prophets effected this transformation: Jeremiah, whose works were read, rewritten and edited,[8] Ezekiel and the Second-Isaiah. When the latter pleaded with the Israelites who were preparing to return to their own country, reminding them that they were "the people who keep the Law in their hearts" (Is. 51:7) and whose "sons have all been taught by Yahweh" (Is. 54:13), he was doing no more than repeating the lessons of Jeremiah's basic oracles (Jer. 31:31-34): the community of the future will be composed of specially gifted members, "clients of Yahweh," whose personal and mystical spirituality will closely resemble his own. Jeremiah referred to himself only once as a "poor man" (*'ebyon* — Jer. 20:13); but he knew how to commit himself totally to God, to make the intimate and trustful surrender that bears fruit in security and joy. This was the lesson of his life. It

[7] "A lowly people of modest means" (Liénart Bible). Wellhausen, on the contrary, describes them as *fromme und demütige Leute.*

[8] Cf. A. Gelin, *Jérémie, Les Lamentations, Baruch* (Paris: 1951), pp. 20-23.

did not escape his friends who, in a triumphant apostrophe, praised Yahweh upon their return from exile:

> Give praise, O you heavens, and rejoice, O earth; you mountains, give praise with jubilation: because Yahweh has comforted his people and has shown mercy to his poor ones (*'aniyyim*) — Is. 49:13.

During the exile the equation of "people" and "poor" became more pronounced. Did it continue when Cyrus allowed the Jews to return home?

The enthusiastic Zionists faced unexpected trials when they tried to re-establish themselves in their ancestral land. Something of the hardship may be guessed when we read about the relative misery in which they were forced to live (Haggai 1:5) and the obstructive measures of the Samaritans.[9a] An attentive observer is surprised by the heterogeneity of Judah's population — half-pagan Judaeo-Benjaminites who had remained in Palestine and who adjusted only with difficulty to the life led by the élite who had gone into exile. Failure marked every effort to convert these "brothers" to a purer form of Yahwism, as it marked every attempt to induce the Jews still in Babylon to return home. All this was part of the formation of a perfect Israel which seems to be the dominant theme of chapters 56–66 of the book of Isaiah.

Recent studies of the Trito-Isaiah, especially those of Elliger,[9b] suggest that these chapters are the work of a single author who sought to provide a solid foundation for the ideal Israel foreseen by Zephaniah and realized during the exile. This community is described in terms that resemble and add a new dimension to the terms Zephaniah used in speaking of the covenant, justice and poverty.

Let us begin with the vocabulary of the covenant. God prepared a "people" for Himself (Is. 60:21; 62:12; 63:8; 65:10, 19, 22; 57:14; 58:1) who would bear an eternal covenant (Is. 61:8). To them were applied traditional names: Yahweh's

[9a] Cf. Alt, "Die Rolle Samarias bei der Entstehung des Judentums," *Festschrift O. Procksch*, pp. 5-28.

[9b] "Der prophet Tritojesaja," *Zeitschrift für Alttestamentliche Wissenschaft*, XLIX (1931), 112-141.

blessed race (Is. 65:9,23), a holy people (Is. 62:12), the elect (Is. 65:9,15,22), the redeemed (Is. 62:12).

Then comes the vocabulary of justice. The term "just" defined the covenant man (Is. 60:21), who confronted "the wicked" (Is. 57:20-21), skeptics (Is. 66:6), idolaters (Is. 57:13), criminals and thieves (Is. 58:6-7; 61:8). Justice (*ṣedaqah*) means fidelity to a religious, moral and social catechism, according to Ezekiel as well as to the Trito-Isaiah. Devout men (Is. 57:1) always possess the fear of God (Is. 57:11), which is a part of justice, or better still, its religious origin. Social obligations are listed with a kind of complacency (Is. 56:10-12; 58:7; 59:4,14ff). Legalism is plain.

But it is the vocabulary of poverty that is central in the vision. Isaiah describes his mission in these words:

> He has sent me to preach to the meek (*ʿanawim*), to heal the contrite of heart, and to preach a release to the captives and deliverance to them that are shut up, to proclaim the acceptable year of Yahweh and the day of vengeance of our God, to comfort all that mourn (Is. 61:1-2).

Here the immediate context points directly to real poverty, as is to be expected in the disillusioning and precarious days of reconstruction. Yet in this picture of the community's physical condition, the word "poor" has a spiritual resonance that can be heard in two precious texts:

> For thus says the High and the Eminent that inhabits eternity. And his name is Holy, who dwells in the high and holy place and with a contrite and humble spirit, to revive the spirit of the humble (*šaphal*) and to revive the heart of the contrite (*daka*) — Is. 57:15.

B. Duhm clearly saw that this denoted, not merely a physical situation, but also "the discouragement that is its result and, among faithful souls, that fervent search for God, prayer, confession, mortification and humility that transforms the 'poor' into the 'pious.' "[10] But this explanation may not satisfy since it is a definition from below,[11] while "poverty"

[10] *Das Buch Jesaia* (Göttingen: 1892), p. 404.

[11] "Demut auf Zeit," according to Elliger, *op. cit.*, pp. 118, 126, 133.

is affirmed in a religious context in which man is situated in the presence of the divine transcendence. This distinction alone explains Isaiah 66:1-2, a sublime passage in which man's littleness when he stands before his God, his fear and trembling when he learns the divine will, are portrayed in a scene that we cannot now identify; perhaps it was the occasion of one of Sheshbazzar's first attempts to reconstruct the sanctuary in Sion:

> Thus says Yahweh: Heaven is my throne, and the earth my footstool. What is this house that you will build to me? And what is this place of my rest? My hand made all these things, and all these things were made, says Yahweh. But to whom shall I have respect, but to him that is poor and little and of a contrite spirit, and that trembles at my words? (Is. 66:1-2).

Spiritual poverty has rarely been so beautifully described: total openness to God, absolute humility, respect, obedience, consciousness of guilt, or better still, compunction.[12] All this points to perfect faith.

The fundamental truths are orchestrated in the postexilic psalms, which were the direct expression of all that the community of the *'anawim* held dear.

In the complex collection known as the psalter are to be found a large number of pre-exilic compositions. The anti-Wellhausian reaction, of which Gunkel's great commentary is a splendid example, has confirmed a number of traditional positions.[13] But it is also true that after the exile the Jews edited and adapted many psalms for use in the second temple.

[12] St. Augustine used this passage from Isaiah in his commentary on the first beatitude as recorded by Matthew. See p. 116. The expression, "he who trembles at the voice of Yahweh," became classic after the exile (Ezra 9:4).

[13] Compare these two assertions: "The question is not whether the psalter contains any postexilic psalms but whether it contains any pre-exilic ones" (Wellhausen); "A great number, I believe I should say by far the greatest number, of psalms date from the pre-exilic period, perhaps at the beginning of this period" (Schmidt).

They rewrote parts of the old "songs of Sion" that they had sung "beside the rivers of Babylon" (Ps. 136:1-4); they also adopted some of the more recent exilic compositions of the Persian period. These spiritual canticles contained the prayers, aspirations, and confessions of religious souls like Jeremiah. In this élite the prophet's soul became, as it were, concretized, and the prophets' dreams were at last realized. These devout men and women were the "remnant," and the "poor," whom Zephaniah, the Second- and the Third-Isaiah had first tried to describe and then to fashion.

It is not our immediate purpose to enter the inner sanctuary of their souls — to do this we would need the help of Jeremiah who has plumbed these depths (*'ebyon*, Jer. 20:13) — but we wish to study their conduct as a group, their awareness that they were, as someone has said, a little church within the Church *(ecclesiola in Ecclesia)*. It was their daring conviction that they constituted the true Israel:

> For Yahweh loves his people, and he adorns the lowly (the *'anawim)* with victory (Ps. 149:4).

This bold parallel inserted in Psalm 149:4 controls the reading of four psalms (33, 36, 9A-9B, 24) of great value to us because they describe the solidarity or communal character of the "movement" of the "poor." All four psalms are alphabetic.[14] Each verse of Psalm 33 begins with one of the twenty-two letters of the Hebrew alphabet. P. Paffrath[15] would have us believe that the true poet was stimulated rather than inhibited by this convention; if he be right, true biblical poets differ very much from Paul Valéry! As a matter of fact, these alphabetic psalms are repetitive and far from perfect literary compositions. But this is precisely what interests us most: in them it is easy to catch the overtones that the word *'anawim* held for a Jew, and the resentment it aroused.

The psalm is highly personalized. An *'ani* received a divine favor and wished to express his gratitude to the Lord

14 Podechard places the four psalms 33, 36, 9A-9B, and 24 in the Persian period.

15 *Die Klagelieder* (Bonn: 1932).

(v. 7). So strong was his sense of community that he invited the other *'anawim* to pray for and rejoice with him. The incident is in a double sense apologetic: from it other "poor men" can learn something more of God's ways, and the wicked who have made them suffer may perhaps be touched. Both groups are reminded that fidelity to Yahweh never goes unrequited. The author becomes a teacher of wisdom for his pupils, but at last a new element breaks the monotony of the patiently repeated lesson and the honorific[16] term expressed in the opening verses is handled thematically and elaborated in seven parallel statements. The poor are "those who fear Yahweh" (vv. 8, 10), "those who find refuge in him" (v. 9), "those who seek him" (v. 11), they are "his holy ones" (v. 10), "the just" (vv. 16, 20, 22), "the brokenhearted" and "souls who have been crushed" (v. 19).

Light is thrown on these last phrases by Psalm 50:19, which is to be understood of spiritual rather than of temporal trials. An editor added an eighth parallel: the "poor" are "the servants of Yahweh" (v. 23). Thus *'anawim* is used as a key-word to the whole religion of the Old Testament, where fear is never far from confidence. When Christ comes, the first — and, in fact, the only — beatitude is to be understood in the light of all others.

Psalm 36 also contains a lesson on wisdom meant for an impatient soul who is shocked by the slow unfolding of divine Providence and has to be counseled: "Wait and see!" Leave it to Yahweh, and wait for him (v. 7). Apparently the admonition is addressed to a young man: let him trust the aphorisms and experience of one of his elders who knows how Yahweh rules the world! God will look after the *'anawim:* "the meek shall possess the land" (v. 11).

Robust optimism of faith can find comfort in enchanting tomorrows but today's "poor" find their lot hard and their situation violent. Yet their name, with its religious connotations, points to no mere sociological status but refers to men

[16] Speaking of words that express the idea of poverty, R. Kittel says that after the exile, it may be observed that "die Wörte sind stolze Ehrenprädikate geworden" (*Die Psalmen,* Leipzig, 1922, p. 286).

"who are subject to Yahweh and obedient to his laws."[17] A study of parallelisms is enlightening: the *ʿanawim* are "those who hope in Yahweh" (v. 9), they are "the righteous" (v. 17 and *passim*), "the innocent" (v. 18), "those blessed by Yahweh" (v. 22), "his faithful ones" (*ḥasidim*, v. 28), "the integrated" and "the peaceful" (v. 37), "those who trust God" (v. 40). In fine, the triple vocabulary of covenant, justice and poverty (found in Trito-Isaiah) is combined to describe "this active band inspired by the same life."[18]

Psalm 9A-9B is a manifesto of the same group. The point of departure is a concrete situation: someone has been saved from disaster (vv. 14-15). The case is seen to be typical; throughout history Yahweh has treated His friends in the same way, and He will do so at the end of the world:

> he has not forgotten the cry of the *ʿanawim*...(9A:13).
>
> The desire of the *ʿanawim* you hear, O Yahweh...(9B:17).

The word *ʿanawim* recurs like a rhyme (9A:14, 19; 9B:2, 9, 12)[19] in the Hebrew text. It describes individuals experiencing specific misfortunes; above all, it evokes their spiritual characteristics. Let us also trust the evidence of parallels: the *ʿanawim* are "those who know the name of Yahweh" (9A:11). Let us also trust the constant antithesis between the "poor," the "impious" and the "proud." We wish to develop this point, convinced as we are that we will never understand the *ʿanawim* unless we understand their opposite numbers.

Psalm 24 is more personal. Yet in its verses we detect the tendency, so congenial to the Jews, towards a reaction both sympathetic and didactic.[20] In a difficult moment the speaker addressed Yahweh with confidence:

> ...for I take refuge in you. Let integrity and uprightness preserve me, because I wait for you, O Lord (v. 21).

[17] E. Podechard, *Le Psautier, traduction littérale et explication historique"* (Lyons: 1949), I, 170.

[18] This is the excellent formula of I. Loeb, *La littérature des pauvres dans la Bible* (Paris: 1892).

[19] Manuscript tradition hesitates between *ʿaniyyim* and *ʿanawim* (9A:13, 19; 9B:12). This is not significant because both terms had acquired a more than sociological meaning during the Persian period.

[20] On this point, see Paul's reflection in Romans 2:17ff.

This was his final word. But in it he alluded to the program of the whole group, finding in it, as it were, support for his own faith. The *'anawim* of verse 9 are "those who make a sincere profession of submission and obedience to God,"[21] that is, those who "keep his covenant and his decrees" (v. 10), who "fear" him (vv. 12, 14), and "hope in him" (v. 3).

In brief, these postexilic psalms trace a well-defined picture of devout and fervent souls who will be known eventually by the almost technical term of *'anawim.* They form "the religious nucleus of the nation."[22] This becomes all the more clear when they are contrasted with their opponents, who constitute an equally distinct group.

To see the *'anawim* as they really were is to see them in the midst of concentric circles of enemies: less fervent Israelites, the ruling classes, men attracted to pagan culture, men filled with a desire for wealth and what St. John will call "the pride of life." The *'anawim,* with some rhetoric and much passion, have left a highly colored picture of these foes, especially of the last group. Their descriptions are vehement but not unjust. They enable us to study the constantly contemporaneous drama of the two cities whose frontiers divide the Chosen People. Contrasted with the *'anawim* are the "wicked" (*raša'*, Ps. 33:22), the "sinners" (*peša'*, Ps. 36:38; *ḥatta'im*, Ps. 24:8), the "proud" (*ge'im*, Ps. 9, *passim*). It is worth noting that this last epithet is used as an antonym for "poor" and profoundly affects its meaning.[23]

More significant than this vocabulary is the concrete conduct of this group composed of men hostile both to the poor (Ps. 9A:14) and to Yahweh (Ps. 36:20). That is precisely the heart of the drama that unfolds between the true Israel and Israel according to the flesh. God has His own witnesses who are "his children" (Ps. 72:15); paradoxically their testimony is given when conditions are at their worst. They never

[21] E. Podechard, *op. cit.,* p. 122.

[22] R. Kittel, *op. cit.,* p. 287.

[23] The word for "the proud" (*ge'im*) appears in the original text of Psalm 9A-9B but has been systematically replaced by the word for "the nations" (*goyim*).

cease crying, protesting, complaining: Why is Yahweh so slow to acknowledge His own?

> Your words have been unsufferable to me, says Yahweh. And you have said: What have we spoken against you? You have said: He labors in vain that serves God, and what profit is it that we have kept his ordinances and that we have walked sorrowful before Yahweh of hosts? Wherefore now we call the proud people happy, for they that work wickedness are built up; and they have tempted God and are preserved.
> Then they that feared the Lord spoke every one with his neighbor, and the Lord gave ear and heard it. And a book of remembrance was written before him for them that fear Yahweh and think on his name.

These words were overheard and transcribed by Malachi (3:13-16) about 430 B.C. These words of the "poor" show that, during the spiritual reawakening of the Persian period, there was "an uncertainty, almost a crisis of faith."[24] In those days men seemed to think that the old law of temporal retribution had only one meaning: by means of a generalization they liberate, as it were, what they, "the right men," considered the great scandal, the misgovernment of the world.

> I was envious of the arrogant when I saw them prosper though they were wicked. For they are in no pain; their bodies are sound and sleek; they are free from the burdens of mortals, and are not afflicted like the rest of men. So pride adorns them as a necklace; as a robe violence enwraps them. Out of their crassness comes iniquity; their fancies overflow their hearts. They scoff and speak evil; outrage from on high they threaten. They set their mouthings in place of heaven, and their pronouncements roam the earth: "So he brings his people to such a pass that they have not even water!" And they say, "How does God know?" and, "Is there any knowledge in the Most High?" (Ps. 72:3-11).

To Job, a literary figure of the "poor" man, are attributed thoughts like the following:

[24] A. Robert, *Les Psaumes,* p. 62.

> Why do the wicked survive, grow old, become mighty in power?... Yet they say to God, "Depart from us, for we have no wish to learn your ways!" (Job 21:7, 14).

A wise old man had observed earlier that it is the satisfied man who disowns God (Prov. 30:9), and Job will not fail to point out that the wicked man who acts boldly before God is always well-fed and successful (Job 15:27). Is this satire? The "poor" man is not known for his humor. He resents "scoffers" *(les)* who do not see what he sees.[25] He is terribly serious because his whole understanding of Providence, his whole religious point of view is involved in this debate in which the adversary always seems to be ahead. In the realm of effective action, human cleverness, uninhibited by scruples, goes much further than the observance of God's law. The children of darkness are more cunning than the sons of light! Unfortunately, the poor and the impious quite spontaneously confront one another in the realm of effective action. Is the possession in this world of what the Bible calls "blessing" *(beraka)*, "peace" *(šalom)*, "salvation" *(yešaʿ)*, a true sign that God loves His own?

Such was the traditional teaching. Yet bolder spirits sneered at such old-fashioned nonsense, because daily experience had shown them that:

> ...he hides his face, he never sees (Ps. 9B:11).

These are the words of a free thinker and they are based on experience. The just man, on the other hand, sees that "reverses," that is, poverty, sickness, prison, exile, are so many divine interventions, a negative theophany (Eliade), an expression of His displeasure, a trial sent from above, an invitation to deeper thought and closer union with Him. The unjust man makes these disasters the theme of his scoffing, mockery and song; they prove that he is safe and that God does not protect His friends.

> All who see me scoff at me; they mock me with parted lips, they wag their heads: "He relied on Yahweh; let him

[25] A. Robert has suggested (*op. cit.*, p. 63) that "psalmist and sage are but two aspects of the same individual; one prays, the other teaches."

> deliver him, let him rescue him, if he loves him" (Ps. 21:8-9).

Since word and act are closely linked in the East, "the slanderer" (Ps. 139:12), the ironic calumniator becomes "the man of blood" (Ps. 25:9; 54:24), ready for violence and criminal attacks, "the troublemaker" (Ps. 93:4).

Two spiritual worlds meet in the psalms, they face and study each other: the wicked who have their reunions and councils, "the assembly of scoffers" (Ps. 1:1) and "the circle of just men" (Ps. 110:1). There is group thinking on both sides. There is also group rejoicing. These opponents hate each other. The sarcasms of the ungodly are matched by the *'anawim's* curses, which ring discordantly in Christian ears but which were meant to be passionate pleas for the re-establishment of divine justice within the limits of retribution in this world.[26]

It is well to insist on this sense of communal solidarity. The *'anawim* loved the *sod* (Ps. 110:1). This word denotes a conversation of friends, a reunion of intimates, a circle of men who confide in each other, rather than an organized society. It is used when referring to the trusting communication of the just with God (Ps. 24:14) and the affection of one creature for another (Ps. 54:15). I. Loeb was right when he did not want to give this expression a too rigidly sociological meaning, although at times he seems to have come very near doing so. "There can be no doubt," he tells us, "that the 'poor' loved to come together, whether in structured groups or not, and that they were particularly happy when they were able to live a communal life with some of their friends, or at least to spend long hours in their company."[27]

[26] For the curses, see Psalms 68 and 108.

[27] *La littérature des Pauvres dans la Bible* (Paris: 1892), pp. 4, 11. Theodore Reinach in his preface to this book speaks with less reserve about the "sect" of the poor (p. vii), and Graetz describes, in his commentary on the psalms (1892), a class of Jews who made a vow of poverty and humility and who probably formed associations or confraternities (p. vii). We shall see that this phenomenon did exist among the Jews but at a later date. See p. 71.

> Behold, how good it is, and how pleasant, where brethren dwell as one! It is as when the precious ointment upon the head runs down over the beard, the beard of Aaron, till it runs down upon the collar of his robe (Ps. 132:1-2).

Saint Augustine once remarked that these words inspired monastic foundations.[28] Here the psalmist is alluding to the "oil of gladness" poured upon the heads of the guests at the banquet's close — the same oil with which the high priests and kings, who were responsible for the prosperity and well-being of the land, were consecrated. This idea of shared happiness is expressed twice in the climate of cultic thanking-services. When one of the *'anawim* escaped from some danger, thus justifying, as it were, the workings of divine Providence, his friends would come to the temple to thank Yahweh for His mercy and to eat a sacred meal. On this fraternal occasion they rejoiced before the Lord:

> The lowly shall eat their fill; they who seek Yahweh shall praise him: "May your hearts be ever merry!" (Ps. 21:27). See, you lowly ones, and be glad; you who seek God, may your hearts be merry! For Yahweh hears the poor, and his own who are in bonds he spurns not (Ps. 68:33-34).[29]

28 PL 37, 1729.

29 "His pious" (*ḥasidim*) should be read instead of "his prisoners" (*'asirim*).

CHAPTER 3

The Spirituality of the "Poor"

The psalter introduces us to the "poor" and enables us to see something of their will-to-community. The ideal Israel, dear to Jeremiah (31:31-34) and Ezekiel (36:24-28), is realized only in them, as they themselves ingenuously declare.[1] So far do they carry this group concept that frequently the mention of their own spiritual experience develops into a description of the Israel which is their spiritual home, the place where their souls thrive (Pss. 129:7-8; 130:3).

We must now study their hidden inner life and discover at what depths they meet their God. Laments, so often repeated that they become monotonous, fill their spiritual canticles.[2] Yahweh blocks their passage, obstructs their paths (Lam. 3:9). The road of life for them is steep, beset with traps and brambles. Words like "misfortune" (*'oni*) and "distress" (*ṣarah*) recur constantly and give their utterances an elegiac tone. They never know success. A strange cortege of various forms of suffering passes before our eyes.

[1] Ps. 149:4; cf. Ps. 72, where Israel is equated with those who are pure of heart (v. 1) or the race (*zera*) of thy children (v. 15).

[2] These psalms, in which laments, acts of confidence and thanksgiving succeed one another, continue and often imitate the "confessions" of Jeremiah. This literary form seems to be spontaneous and may include individual lamentations (3, 5, 6, 7, 12, 16, 21, 24, 25, 26, 27, 30, 31, 34, 35, 37, 38, 41, 42, 50, 53, 54, 55, 56, 58, 60, 62, 63, 68, 69, 70, 85, 87, 100, 101, 108, 119, 129, 139, 140, 141, 142) and the psalms of confidence (4, 10, 11, 15, 22, 26, 51, 61, 114, 120, 124, 125, 130, 138).

Literary works of antiquity are usually focused on rulers and important men — *humanum paucis vivit genus;* it was reserved for the Bible to evoke the great theory of little people who move through history and who disturb the tranquil lives of other men with their cries. Theirs is the blood of Abel that has been heard from the early days of the human race, theirs is a place in the crowds on whom Christ will have pity, theirs are the laments preserved in the old psalter. Echoing the complaints of Malachi 3:5 and Nehemiah 5:1-5, the psalmists record the results of social injustice in the lives of men whom the insolent rich vex and wicked judges deceive. Perhaps we may also detect in these psalms the voice of Levites, whose position may then have been in jeopardy (Neh. 13:10-11; Pss. 5:9; 26:11-12).[3]

The number of sick is particularly large and E. Podechard gives us a vivid picture of their experience: "The plight of the sick man delights his enemies. They taunt him (21:8), insult him (101:9), rejoice over his imminent death (40:8-9), long for the end of his life (21:18-19), hope it will come soon (40:3-6), do all that they can to hasten it (21:13-14, 17, 21-22). There is something impious about their attitude (21:9; 37:21): they are happy to see that when he is brought low Yahweh is powerless to assist him. Their malevolent joy grieves the psalmists (21:7; 29:2; 37:17; 40:12; 101:9). The hostility of these wicked men is all too plain in moments of trial. They are not moved to pity, they respect neither his misfortune nor his weakness (cf. 37:20).

"At such crises even his friends may desert the poor man (37:12). Even though they may have broken bread with him, they do not hesitate to raise their foot to kick him (40:10). If we remind ourselves that we are considering an age less individualistic than our own, when dependence on the group, morally as well as materially, was greater than it is now and the private life of the individual was not as secret or as free as it can be today, if we recall that loss of prestige involved greater humiliation and every kind of inconvenience, we will better understand

[3] This is the hypothesis of Graetz-Renan.

the laments of a hypersensitive man whose imagination made the situation seem worse than it really was."[4]

To all these sufferings we must add the anguish of imprisonment that so disturbs the heroes of Psalms 21 and 68, as well as the widespread hostility that confronts the author of Psalm 119, who is forced to dwell among the barbarians of the far north or the east:

> Woe is me that I sojourn in Mosoch, that I dwell amid the tents of Cedar! All too long have I dwelt with those who hate peace (vv. 5-6).

Must we repeat (Loeb[5] to the contrary) that these fervent souls never take pleasure in their misfortunes or become reconciled to them? *Vita vivere in terra viventium* expresses their heart's desire; they look forward to earthly retribution in terms of "life," "joy," "light," "blessing," "peace," "security," "salvation."[6] If the law of retribution seems not to be operative in their case, they weigh the possibility of their guilt, they examine their conscience and do not cease to acknowledge their sin, which they believe explains their situation:

> For all about me are evils beyond reckoning; my sins so overcome me that I cannot see; they are more numerous than the hairs of my head, and my heart fails me (Ps. 39:13).

In time the repeated enumeration and classification of their sins became a discouraging and disappointing occupation. This did not mean that they ceased to believe that misfortunes were the consequence of sin — nothing could persuade them to the contrary. But they began to wonder why God exacted so much of His friends. They had no theology of substitution but they did think that absolute faith is a straight path to God.

Yes, human reverses point to sin; but, going deeper, might they not be the painful means chosen by God to lead man to total surrender, to a form of denudation in His presence, to a

[4] *Revue Biblique*, 1920, pp. 53-54.

[5] I. Loeb, *op. cit.*, p. 21; likewise Causse, *op. cit.*, p. 100. It also appears unexpectedly in Gauthier's fine study, *Magnanimité* (Paris: Vrin, 1951), p. 384.

[6] These terms are all found in Psalm 84.

dramatic purification of faith that would culminate in the cry: *"De profundis clamavi ad te, Domine!"*? "Suffering does not diminish us but reveals us to ourselves.... There are thresholds that thought, left to its own resources, can never cross; an experience is needed, poverty, sickness.... It is as if our eyes are opened and we can see things that we never even dreamed. Perhaps the world itself is given another dimension,"[7] the vertical dimension, that short journey that leads straight from misfortune to the invocation:

> I am miserable (*'ani*) and poor (*'ebyon*)!
> Hasten, Yahweh;
> You are my help and savior,
> My God, do not delay!

This was the route traversed by Jeremiah the prophet, who was the predecessor of the *'anawim* and their inspiration. No need to repeat here his tale of woe.[8] His vocation was to suffer. Few of his intractable audience would listen to him and his sarcasm alienated them still further. He had scarcely any disciples and no home of his own to which he could turn for support. He was denounced by the men of his village, by priests and official prophets, by Judean officials. Disputes, persecution, reverses are the substance of his "Confessions," from which our *'anawim* will borrow form, vocabulary and pattern.[9] But amid the cries of distress can be heard affirmations of faith, for which the trials themselves provided, as it were, a springboard. Making use of a cliché found in the psalms of the sick, Jeremiah cries:

> Heal me, Yahweh, and I shall be healed; Save me, and I shall be saved; for you are my praise (Jer. 17:14).

After his recriminations against divine Providence, at the height of the crisis in which he began to question and then to accept more perfectly his own vocation, the prophet was told by the Lord to silence his too human complaints, those com-

7 G. Marcel, *Le Chemin de Crète*, p. 174.
8 See our "Jérémie" in *Témoins de Dieu* (Paris: 1952), pp. 103-117.
9 *Ibid.*, pp. 183-186.

plaints which were to be the consolation of his disciples throughout the centuries:

> ...and if you will separate the precious from the vile, you shall be as my mouth (Jer. 15:19).

Yahweh no more intended to justify His ways now than He did a few years earlier (Jer. 12:5). There was no question of debating a point of justice with Him (Jer. 12:1). The only possible religious attitude is silence in the presence of the mystery of divine justice, the silence of faith.

> For I am with you to save you and to deliver you, says the Lord (Jer. 15:20).

Is this not the essential certitude given by God to His servant? Thus Jeremiah, the poor man (*'ebyon*, Jer. 20:13), learned to commit himself totally to God in a complete, light-giving act of faith. "When in this world we struggle towards God, believing that we are following Him, yet failure crowns our efforts, only one immeasurable reality remains: God is."[10]

Similar sentiments can be found in a complex composition that we date at the close of the exile and that Rudolph has entitled *Das Vorbild Jeremia.* This third lamentation is the work of one of the prophet's disciples who takes his place among *'anawim* writers. No mere imitator, he makes a contribution of his own.[11] Using the clichés of his anthologic style, he analyzes the heart-rending experiences of his master. His sorrow is an expression of grief over his own sufferings as well as those of his country:

> Remember my poverty and transgression, the wormwood and the gall. I will be mindful and remember; and my soul shall languish within me (Lam. 3:19-20).

Suddenly there is a change of tone. He understands that a religious silence is the perfect response, the expression of his inner attitude of unconditional faith:

> Yahweh is my portion, said my soul; therefore will I wait for him....It is good to wait with silence for the salvation

[10] Karl Jaspers, *Introduction à la philosophie* (Paris: 1951), p. 54.
[11] See our article: "Lamentations de Jérémie," *Supplément au Dictionnaire de la Bible,* Vol. V, col. 246.

> of God. . . . He shall sit solitary and hold his peace, because he has taken it upon himself. He shall put his mouth in the dust; if so, there may be hope[12] (Lam. 3:24, 26, 28-29).

These words bring us to Job's final attitude. Of small importance is the question of the historical identity of this figure of the past whom a poet and a genius has made the subject of his immortal poem. Such a problem can hold no interest for one who has grasped the meaning of the book. The monologues and dialogues of God's friend are classic because they are heavy with the anonymous experience of each one of the *'anawim,* and they are as true as the "confessions" of Jeremiah. "The special merit of the book of Job is that it gives us in both literature and theology . . . a type of the poor."[13]

Job is a more colorful Jeremiah. Misfortunes are piled upon him. Jeremiah described God as one who has deceived and vanquished him (Jer. 20:7); Job calls Him an enemy and assailant (16:12; 19:12), who allowed him no chance to be alone (7:19) or to draw breath (9:19), a kind of blind force (14:13, 18-19) whose power is more patent than His equity. Yet faith prevails. Praying and hoping, Job comes to the realization that God's justice is a mystery that does not correspond to any of the usual categories. Contemporary theologians were distressed because they feared he was "doing away with piety" (15:4), while in reality he was safeguarding it by moving into the transcendent dimension, access to God Himself — *ipsissimus Deus* — that goes beyond "representations" and "images."

At the same time he perceived that man can never claim to be pure in the sight of his Creator, yet he cannot help asking why God exacts so much from His creature. He faces a double mystery: divine transcendence and human misery. His faith, undiminished and purified, brings this long debate to an end. Job does not come to his conclusion "as a result of reasoning but as a result of the intensity of the religious sentiment that

[12] Notice, in connection with the theme of silence, the translation of "contrite heart," in Isaiah 66:2, by *hesychios*, "calm," "pacified."
[13] A. Robert, *Les Psaumes*, p. 49.

sustains him. In this way the poem reaches a religious solution: man should trustingly submit to God and believe in Him even though his mind can find no solace."[14]

> I know that you can do all things, and that no purpose of yours can be hindered. I have dealt with great things that I do not understand, things too wonderful for me which I cannot know. I had heard of you by word of mouth, but now my eye has seen you. Therefore I disown what I have said, and repent in dust and ashes (Job 42:2-6).

This silence, this contrition, this humility, this total commitment, this "absolute recourse" is the essential attitude of the poor. The theme may vary according to temperaments and situations, but the same infinite credit is always extended to God. This we see in Psalm 130, where Origen, in his treatise against Celsus,[15] was able to discover a biblical climate unlike Hellenic wisdom:

> Yahweh, my heart is not proud, nor are my eyes haughty; I busy not myself with great things, nor with things too sublime for me. Nay, rather, I have stilled and quieted my soul like a weaned child. Like a weaned child on its mother's lap, (so is my soul within me). O Israel, hope in Yahweh, both now and forever (Ps. 130:1-3).

Whatever form misfortune may have taken in the lives of these men — be it the misery (*'oni*) or distress (*ṣarah*) to which they refer so frequently, or simply the disillusionment experienced by the discreet psalmist to whom we have listened — it is very plain that this misfortune has showed them the way to God:

> Before I was afflicted (*'e'aneh*) I went astray (Ps. 118:67).

"Suffering acquired a dignity; it was understood now to be a road leading to the divine. It has nothing in common with the fatalism of Greek tragedy as we see it in the story of the Servant of Yahweh (Second-Isaiah) and in the symbol of the Cross. Biblical religion does not know the limitations of the

14 Larcher, *Le livre de Job* (Paris: 1950), p. 23.
15 Origen, *Contra Celsum*, III, 62f., 71.

tragic conscience, or rather it has gone beyond them."[16] One day the author of the epistle to the Hebrews will say of Christ: "Son though he was, he learned obedience from the things that he suffered." According to a recent commentator, this sentence enables us to understand the Hebrew term *'anawah*,[17] to which we will return. It also expresses the dialectic of the Old Testament that transformed human derelicts into clients of Yahweh. In them Yahweh could find the "crevice," the receptivity[18] that St. Paul describes in terms of hearing (Gal. 3:2). Unlimited confidence (expressed by the key-words *batah, qawah, yihel,* which express hope) and joyous, radical humility — all this is contained in the *'anawah* concept.

Along the spiritual journey that we have just described, we find, like so many landmarks, words denoting poverty in its many modalities. The psalter is studded with them, and, it may be added, they have been inserted in its verses with discrimination. To pause here is imperative.

'ani, 'ebyon, dal are the first words that occur to the psalmists when they wish to portray the misery of their condition:[19]

> . . . for I am wretched (*'ani*) and poor (*'ebyon*), and my heart is pierced within me. Like a lengthening shadow I pass away (Ps. 108:22-23).

> But I am afflicted and in pain; let your saving help, O God, protect me (Ps. 68:30).

> All my being shall say, "Yahweh, who is like you, the rescuer of the afflicted man (*'ani*) from those too strong for him, of the afflicted and the needy (*'ebyon*) from their despoilers?" (Ps. 34:10).

> Incline your ear, Yahweh; answer me, for I am afflicted (*'ani*) and poor (*'ebyon*). Keep my life, for I am devoted to you; save your servant who trusts in you (Ps. 85:1-2).

16 Karl Jaspers, *La foi philosophique* (Paris: 1952), p. 54.

17 C. Spicq, *L'Épître aux Hébreux*, II, 1953, p. 117.

18 This is why W. Sattler in *Die 'anawim im Zeitalter Jesu Christi* (Tübingen: 1927) will define the "poor" as those who are waiting (*prosdechomenoi*): Matthew 15:43; Luke 2:25, 38.

19 To this list should be added *dak* (oppressed) and *šaphal* (abased).

> May the humble *(dak)* not retire in confusion; may the afflicted *(ʿani)* and the poor *(ʾebyon)* praise your name (Ps. 73:21).

It has been pointed out that these lines contain an ardent and habitual reference to the God who saves. There is something pathetic in the way these men do not hesitate to use violent terms when describing their position, convinced as they are that God is on their side. In fact, as we have already seen,[20] they go so far as to claim that they belong among the just:

> I know that Yahweh renders justice to the afflicted *(ʿani)*, judgment to the poor *(ʾebyon)*. Surely the just shall give thanks to your name; the upright shall dwell in your presence (Ps. 139: 13-14).

But it is most characteristic that they are opposed to the proud *(zed, geʾah, ram)*. This antithesis made so insistently (Ps. 9A-9B, 85, 93, 118, 122) places them at once in a religious climate:

> For lowly people you save *(am-ʿani)* but haughty eyes you bring low *(ramoth)* — (Ps. 17:28).
>
> ...be not forever unmindful of the lives of your afflicted ones *(ʿaniyyim)* — (Ps. 73:19).
>
> For Yahweh hears the poor *(ʾebyonim)*, and his own who are in bonds he spurns not (Ps. 68:34).

Behind these appeals and affirmations can we not find something more than the assurance that the speaker will emerge safely from a difficult trial? Are they not the expression of the soul's complete surrender and total commitment to God? There is a word that conveys this idea: *ʿanaw* is the privileged title of one "who is not sly or shrewd" with God, and the corresponding virtue, *ʿanawah,* has all the resonances of humility. Exact equivalents do not seem to exist in other languages. This is always true of terms denoting rich spiritual experiences, e.g., Pauline "faith," or "Olierian" adoration. Such expressions have a certain aura all their own, and we have seen in an

20 Cf. above, p. 19.

earlier chapter how *'anaw* eventually became a synonym for a religious man.

The Greek translator of the psalter felt that he had to break new ground, so he used two words with noble overtones: *praüs,* meaning gentle, merciful, peaceful, and *praütes,* gentleness, benevolence. In this choice he seems to have made more explicit a latent meaning, because *'anaw* is a man who stands before Yahweh "trembling at His word," obedient to His orders, welcoming His gifts, admittedly disconcerted by His blows, well aware of his own sinfulness and weakness, but always sure that he is Yahweh's child. Little by little this man, through a kind of living logic, will reach an inner peace, a special kind of patience, even an understanding of other men. All this is implied in the Old Testament but not until the New Testament will it be completely explicated.[21]

Other Greek words were available but the translator did not think that they conveyed the religious dimension of the Hebrew vocabulary of poverty; that is why, as a rule, he used them only to describe the psalmists' sociological condition. So *'ani, 'ebyon, dal* became *penes, ptochos,* and *tapeinos.*

Aristophanes says in *Plutus* (552-553): "To live the life of *ptochos* of which you speak, is to live possessing nothing; to live the life of *penes,* on the contrary, is to live frugally and circumspectly." The former is the life of a beggar seeking alms, the latter that of a man barely able to make ends meet. The Greek translator of the psalter ennobled both words, in-

[21] C. Spicq, "Bénignité, mansuétude, douceur, clémence," *Revue Biblique,* 1947, pp. 324-332, contains a good analysis of *'anawah-praütes.* The essential element of *praütes* is humility .... The *praüs* is the Israelite who understands God, His goodness, His justice, His providence and who accepts God's will in its totality. He is docile when God commands, receptive when God teaches. In conjunction with *'emunah* (fidelity), *praütes* denotes a trustful dependence, an untroubled, humble abandonment to God that might be translated by "*disponibilité.*" Gauthier (*op. cit.,* pp. 377, 401) stressed another aspect of *'anawah,* openness to others, "humility to one's neighbor." The experience of compunction best reveals this dimension. This disposition is free from hardness of heart, indulgence, a hail-fellow-well-met attitude in daily life. The parable of the Pharisee and the publican makes clear that fraternal humility is the true test of humility before God. — For an exhaustive commentary on *'anawah,* see P. Voillaume, *Seeds of the Desert* (London: 1955).

vesting them with the meaning of *'anaw* (Ps. 21:27; 68:33). But few followed his example.

Nor did Hellenic writers ennoble *tapeinos*. In their works it suggests littleness, lowliness. "I fear that Lysias seems to lack breadth of vision *(tapeinos phane),*" we read in Plato's *Phaedra* (257); and Aristotle (*Politics* 4:11) thinks of the *tapeinos* as a man stripped of all the usual blessings, such as success, strength, riches, friends. Yet in one beautiful passage of the *Laws*, Plato uses the word in all its new nobility:

> God, as the old tradition declares, holding in his hand the beginning, middle, and end of all that is, travels according to his nature in a straight line towards the accomplishment of his end. Justice always accompanies him, and is the punisher of those who fall short of the divine law. To justice, he who would be happy holds fast, and follows in her company with all humility and order *(tapeinos kai kekosmemenos)*; but he who is lifted up with pride, or elated by wealth or rank, or beauty, who is young and foolish, and has a soul hot with insolence *(hybris)*, and thinks that he has no need of any guide or ruler, but is able himself to be the guide of others, he, I say, is left deserted of God.[22]

Here, wisdom that is moderate and modest is placed above *hybris* or excess. This is not humility, the recognition of one's relation to the sovereign and merciful God, with the lively realization of personal powerlessness and inability to please, which makes a man open with his neighbor. Perfection in Greek eyes is a personal adjustment of balance and order; to the biblical man it is the result of a drama in which the personal God and His creature each take part: the creature accepts an invitation — this is *'anawah;* the creature refuses — this is sin. Balance by definition is limited. *'anawah* knows no limits, because its dimensions are the dimensions of God.[23]

[22] *Laws*, 715c-716b (*Dialogues of Plato*, II, trans. B. Jowett). For pagan and Christian reactions to this passage, see E. des Places, S. J., "La tradition indirecte des Lois de Platon (I-VI), *Mélanges J. Saunier* (Lyons: 1944), pp. 34-35.

[23] H. Cremer, *Biblisch-theologisches Wörterbuch der Neutestamentlicher Gräcität* (Gotha: 1895), p. 924.

The Greeks say gloomy and pessimistic things about the individual who stands in the presence of the gods.[24] Yet Hellenism seems to have reached the conclusion that a prayerful and humble attitude pleases the gods, who "in the twinkling of an eye can crush the mighty and with utmost ease rescue the lowly man *(mikroi)* from the greatest dangers." These are the words Xenophon addressed to his troops after they had made a vow *(Anabasis* III, 2, 10; cf. VI, 3, 18). He comes close to the idea of humility but he does not use the word *tapeinos.* It is true that when *tapeinos* is used in the Greek psalter,[25] it does not always have a religious connotation; but its nobility cannot be questioned in Psalm 17:28 cited above, and in Psalm 130:2 where the "silence" of soul in the Hebrew text is given the enriched translation: "I kept my soul in humility."

This investing of Greek terms with new and fuller meaning is less apparent in the psalter than in other books of the Bible. Yet it is interesting to observe that post-Septuagint translators did not hesitate to transform sociological terms. Let us examine Psalm 17:28:

> ...for lowly *(am-'ani)* people you save....

The Septuagint translated *'ani* by *tapeinos;* Aquila used *penes;* Symmachus *praüs.*[26] The whole vocabulary of poverty is, as it were, promoted. We must not fail to recall this when we read the first beatitude in Luke, "Blessed are the poor *(ptochoi).*"

Contemporary manuscripts, especially in Hebrew, show how slowly this vocabulary evolved. In Psalm 9A-9B, the "canticle *par excellence* of the poor and humble,"[27] is refer-

[24] Here we must mention the old theme that Aesop expressed this way: "God lowers what is lofty and lifts what is lowly" (Diogenes Laertes, *Vit. philos.,* I, 69). The same idea is also found in the Babylonian creation epic *(Enuma elish,* tab. IV, 8): "Let the power of lowering *(šaphalu)* and raising be in thy hand" (Marduk). It will recur in the *Magnificat.* Paganism believed that the gods were acting arbitrarily when they did these things; the moral monotheism of the Bible handled the theme very differently.

[25] For example, Psalm 87:16.

[26] For the Greek translations of the Old Testament, see Origen's *Hexapla* in Field's edition, 2 vol., Oxford.

[27] Gauthier, *op. cit.,* p. 388.

ence made (9A:13, 19; 9B:13, 17) to *'aniyyim*, the oppressed and unfortunate, or to *'anawim*, the humble and open to God? The Greek use of *penes* and *ptochos* would incline us to adopt the first reading, as is the case in several Hebrew manuscripts for 9B:17 and the Masoretic text for 9A:19. Yet it is significant that the latter gives us the following lines for 9A:13 and 9B:13, 17.

> (Yahweh) has not forgotten the cry of the afflicted.... Forget not the afflicted! ...The desire of the afflicted you hear, O Lord.

Our investigation, so far, has been limited to the psalter. Despite a general uniformity of vocabulary, certain modifications can be detected; these are more pronounced in other books of the Bible. Two conclusions may be drawn:

a) Spiritual attitudes find apt expression in Hebrew. Sometimes it is easy to discern a transition from a sociological to a religious meaning, for example in Psalm 9A-9B and in *qere-ketib* passages.[28] Elsewhere, all traces of transition have vanished: *'ani, 'ebyon*, and *dal* were part of the religious vocabulary from the beginning, as we have seen in Zephaniah 3:12.[29]

b) Transformations in the Greek text are equally startling. "The Septuagist gave the word *ptochos* the religious value of equivalent Hebrew words. Besides, the Greek language provided no clearer term: *tapeinos* (vile and low) sometimes was used in a pejorative sense, but ordinarily it meant merely a social level which could also be denoted by *ptochos*. Its moral and religious value was also derived from the Septuagint and precisely because it translated the same Hebrew words as *ptochos*."[30]

[28] This term denotes marginal notations of doubtful biblical readings. Rabbinic editors used *ketib*, meaning what is written; *qere*, what should be read.

[29] See pp. 29-31. No explanation has been found for the fact that *'ani*, patently used in a religious sense here, loses this meaning in the psalter and later texts.

[30] Gauthier, *op. cit.*, p. 398.

A few examples will illustrate this. In Isaiah 66:2[31] it is said that Yahweh looked down on the humble (*'ani*); the Septuagint translated *'ani* by *tapeinos,* Aquila by *praüs,* Symmachus by *ptochos.*

Proverbs 3:31-35 contain the admonitions that preface the collection of maxims and repeat the parallelisms we know so well: "the just" = "the right" = "the wise" = "the humble." (God) gives His grace to the humble (*qere: 'anawim; ketib: 'aniyyim*). The Septuagint continues to use *tapeinos.*

The oldest collection of proverbs attributed to Solomon contains a critique of pride (*ga'on, hybris*) that ends with this sentence:

> It is better to be humble (*šaphal-ruḥ*) with the meek (qere: *'anawim;* ketib: *'aniyyim*), than to share plunder with the proud (*ge'im*) — Prov. 16:19.

In the Septuagint the same words are translated this way:

> Of greater worth is the man who is humble of heart (*praüthumos*) than the meek man (*tapeinos*) who divides booty with the proud.

Isaiah (29:19) opens the perspectives of salvation to the just in these words:

> And the meek (*'anawim*) shall increase their joy in the Lord, and the poor men (*'ebyonim*) shall rejoice in the Holy One of Israel.

The Septuagint translated the first word by *ptochos;* Aquila, Symmachus and Theodotion used *praüs.* The second word was glossed in the Septuagint as "those without hope"; Aquila and Theodotion used *endees.*

Isaiah, in one of the poems of his Apocalypse, tells of haughty villagers who tread upon the humble (*'ani*) and the poor (*dal*). The Septuagint, stressing the spiritual note, used *praüs* (Theodotion: *penes*) and *tapeinos.*

Zephaniah was the first to use *'anawah* when referring to humility and the sapiential writers were quick to adopt his word. Three times in old collections of proverbs it was

[31] See above, p. 34.

compared with wisdom or fear of God and was contrasted with pride, as if it were the foundation of religion itself. Zephaniah paralleled it with justice (Zeph. 2:3). Micah (6:8)[32] and Isaiah (2:6-22)[33] did not know the word but point to the reality it denotes as the logical conclusion and crown of faith.

> The reward of humility (*'anawah)* an fear of Yahweh is riches, honor and life (Prov. 22:4).
>
> The fear of Yahweh is training for wisdom, and humility (*'anawah)* goes before honors (Prov. 15:33).
>
> Before his downfall a man's heart is haughty, but humility (*'anawah)* goes before honors (Prov. 18:12).

The wise man always speaks in terms of earthly happiness. This happiness can be purchased with the coin of virtue, but this virtue must be understood in terms of its origin. Ben Sirach, the comfortable middle-class citizen of second-century Jerusalem, made the word *'anawim* the center of one of those shrewd slogans that he so much wished to teach to rich and poor. Like a truly wise man, he studied other men, he excoriated the wicked wealthy man (Sir. 13:18-19) and the impious and idle poor man (13:23; 10:27); to both he offered much advice, so conscious was he of social realities and tradition. But his judgments of men were based on higher values.

> Be it tenant or wayfarer, alien or pauper, his glory is the fear of God. It is not just to despise a man who is wise but poor, nor proper to honor any sinner. The prince, the ruler, the judge are in honor; but none is greater than he who fears God (Sir. 10:21-23).

To fear God means primarily to be mindful of one's human situation.

> My son, with humility (*'anawah)* have self-esteem (Sir. 10:27).

[32] "O man, you have been told what is right, what Yahweh demands of you — nothing else than to act with justice, to love with tenderness, to walk humbly with your God."

[33] See p. 115.

> The abomination of pride (*ge'ah*) is humility (*'anawah*) (cf. 13:20).

He described the basic attitude of a religious man in 1:27:

> What (the Lord) loves is faith and humility (*praütes*).

Only a nuance separates one from the other: faith includes humility, docility and receptivity. In the eulogy of the fathers that he incorporated in his sacred history, Ben Sirach praised Moses:

> For his trustworthiness (*'emunah*) and meekness (*'anawah*) God selected him from all mankind (Sir. 45:4).

The terms are taken from Numbers 12:3-7 and throw light on the meaning of this difficult passage.[34] Therefore:

> More and more, humble (*šaphal*) your pride (*ga' awah*) (Sir. 7:17).

> Insolence (*ga' awah*) is not allotted to a man (Sir. 10:18).

Humility is radiant with goodness and friendliness:

> Give a hearing to the poor man (*'ani*), and return his greeting with humility (*'anawah*) — Sir. 4:8.

> My son, conduct your affairs with humility (*'anawah*), and you will be loved more than a giver of gifts. Humble yourself the more, the greater you are, and you will find favor with God. For great is the mercy of God; to the humble (*'anawim*) he reveals secrets (*sod*) — Sir. 3:17-19.[35]

Not the least of Ben Sirach's charms is his anticipation of the Gospel words used in speaking of the revelation of the mystery of the kingdom:

> I praise you, Father, Lord of heaven and earth, that you did hide these things from the wise and prudent, and did reveal them to little ones (*nepioi*) — Luke 10:21.

[34] See pp. 60-61.

[35] All the citations from Ben Sirach are taken from the Hebrew text. See I. Lévi, *L'Ecclésiastique ou la sagesse de Jésus, fils de Sira* (Paris: Leroux, 1898, 1901). In every instance *'anawah* is translated by *praütes*. Where the Hebrew text is defective in 1:27, no doubt *praütes* is to be understood.

It has been said that Ben Sirach disengaged the religious attitude of the *ʿanawah* "from the material substructure in which it first appeared. The social condition no longer mattered; humility became but an inner attitude of soul, a moral ideal accessible to all men, to rich and poor."[36] With this statement we agree perfectly. According to Zephaniah, *ʿanawah* was a virtue that had its place in a more concrete context.[37] But we may ask if this context is not necessary to the development of this virtue. Is "spiritual poverty" possible without the "poor poverty" of which Msgr. Ancel speaks? So necessary is this "poor poverty" that more than a century after Ben Sirach, those skilled in the practice of *ʿanawah* protect this virtue by something that very much resembles a vow of poverty.[38]

J. van der Ploeg was the first to suggest a significant rapprochement between *ʿanawah* and *islam,* between *ʿanaw* and *muslim.*[39] The technical religious meaning of *islam* is submission. "Quite repugnant to the natural tendency of the Arab soul is the attitude of humble and trusting submission on which the religion in the Koran is based."[40] In it Abraham is presented as the model of the religious man, the *muslim,* the man-subject-to-God, the true believer of divine revelation. The origin of this word is, in fact, attributed to the patriarch: "It is he who has called you, *al muslimi*" (Sourate 22:77).

At last the *ʿani-ʿanaw* ideal was incarnated in the great biblical heroes of every century. This was done in the years

36 Gauthier, *op. cit.,* p. 396.

37 See p. 30.

38 See p. 71.

39 "Les pauvres d'Israël, *Oudtestamentische Studiën,* VII, p. 267.

40 Youakim Moubarac, "Islam et paix," *Dieu vivant,* 23, p. 89. The author gives these definitions: "*Islam* essentially, according to the many aspects proposed by the original Arabs, is a *state of peace,* due, through God's grace, to a total *submission* to Him, by means of a previous *abandonment* and, as it were, *surrender.* The *musulman* is one who has laid aside his weapons in order to trust in God alone and in Him to find protection and security. *A'uzu bi'l-lah!* (I seek refuge in God!) This is not a *traditor,* but a true *traditio sui,* an unconditional surrender of self to God, the master of Peace" (p. 87). See also the work of the same author, "Abraham en Islam," *Cahiers Sioniens,* 2 (1952), pp. 104ff.

after the exile when this ideal was fully understood. In a composite liturgical psalm, recalling the foundation of that Jerusalem sanctuary and the dynastic promise of 2 Samuel 7, the community began its prayer with these words:

> Be mindful, Yahweh, of David and all his misfortunes (*'unnot*).

A "rereading" attested by the Septuagint replaced "misfortunes" with "humility" (*'anawah, praütes*), that is to say, a certain modality of his piety.

But there is more than this. When titles were given to the psalms, after the exile, and an attempt was made to associate them with incidents of the past, King David, because of his unfailing faith during many trials, became something like an "epic hero" of the poor. The titles of the psalms may indeed be highly significant; they attest David's greatness and cast a messianic aura about him.[41] Surely it is in this climate that we should situate the religious title of *'ani* given to his descendant in Zechariah 9:9.[42] "Of the sixty-nine times *'ani* is used in the psalms, thirty-five occur in psalms attributed to David. This can be explained by the fact that he, like the poor, was afflicted and oppressed; also, these misfortunes enabled him to understand something of the gratuity of God's action in his life; and, lastly, the way of poverty was his way of entering royal glory."[43]

"Moses was an exceedingly humble man (*'anaw, praüs*); no one more humble could be found on earth." Is this reflection of Numbers 12:3 a gloss, as Sellin claims? Most exegetes would admit that it is, at least, a later Elohistic addition, as are the next four verses (5-8) where Moses is praised as the prototype of all prophets. Here we can be sure that *'anaw* has a religious meaning. Spicq explains: "We see that he is humbly submissive to God's orders, yet obdurate towards Pharaoh, whose heart was hardened and absolutely unrespon-

[41] Compare the longing for the messiah-David in Ezek. 34:24; 36:25.
[42] See p. 90.
[43] T. Maertens, "Le vocabulaire des béatitudes," *Lumière et Vie,* 8 (1952), p. 22.

sive to God's desires, and he was also opposed to the intractable Israelites when they murmured against God."[44]

Not until Abraham do we find anyone honored as "patron of the poor." In the *Pirke Aboth (The Sayings of the Fathers)*, which goes back in part to the days just before the coming of Christ, a contrast is made between a disciple of Abraham and one of Balaam: "A kindly eye, a humble *(šaphal)* soul and the attitude of a poor *(namokah)* man are characteristic of Abraham's disciple; but a disciple of Balaam has a critical eye, a disdainful *(rahab)* soul and his attitude is haughty *(gebuha)*."[45]

We shall now apply this title to the Messiah. But before we trace this new development of our theme we must examine its communal values in the next chapter.

[44] *Revue Biblique*, 1947, *art. cit.*, p. 326.

[45] *Pirke Aboth* V, 29, ed. C. Taylor (Cambridge: 1897), p. 94. According to rabbinic tradition, words derived from *'anaw* (humility-meekness) were applied to Hillel (*Aboth* of R. Nathan, XV, ed. S. Schlechter [London: 1887], p. 60). See J. Bonsirven, *Le Judaïsme palestinien au temps de Jésus-Christ*, II (1935), pp. 275-280.

CHAPTER 4

The Church of the "Poor" in the Last Centuries of Judaism

During the final centuries of Judaism the psalms continued to shape Jewish piety and provide a mystical orientation of which "poverty" was an essential element. When the psalter was translated into Greek, as we have tried to show, the connotation of many of its Hebrew words was enlarged. Additional proof for this claim may be found in translations of other books of the Bible. The conclusion is inescapable that in the Septuagint *penes, ptochos, tapeinos,* as well as *praüs,* acquired values that made it possible to use them to describe the conduct of the "biblical man" in God's sight and to lay foundations for Christian expression of faith.[1]

An examination of Greek translations of the Old Testament made on Jewish soil after the completion of the translation of the Septuagint shows that the spiritual values of the vocabulary of poverty had been accepted.[2] This can also be verified in the apocrypha which will be discussed in this chapter. Since most of the original Hebrew texts are no

[1] All the translators of the Septuagint (known under the legendary title of "the Seventy") do not seem to have followed the same principles in finding Greek equivalents for Hebrew words. Monographs on this topic for each book of the Bible are much to be desired. For the purposes of our study, however, the conclusions we have reached seem valid.

[2] See pp. 55-56.

longer extant, the Semitic terms hidden behind the Greek words can only be conjectured, but it seems certain that in both languages the words were understood in a religious sense.

The citation of both biblical and parabiblical texts should occasion no surprise. To study a theme thoroughly, every link of the chain must be understood. God's people are on the march; they are living through their catechumenate; their tradition is a developing one; therefore we welcome everything that can help us to reconstruct their history — the inspired text where it is established, "rereadings" of this text as they were made from time to time, the influence of this text and the forms of religious life for which it served as foundation. "It follows immediately that it is a task of primary importance for Catholic theology to consider with much more precision and, should I say, with much more sympathy than it has up to this time, this nebula of the final Jewish tradition in which the Christian universe and Christ Himself were born."[3]

Jewish tradition after this time was transmitted in Greek. The foundation of Alexandria in 332 opened up extraordinary possibilities for Judaism. Supported by Alexander and the Ptolemies, the Jews established in the new Athens a loyal community, specially skilled in finance and at times so provokingly proud that pagan historians applied to them the word *amixia,* meaning "reserved" or "aloof." They easily made Hellenistic culture their own, accepted its philosophy, did not hesitate to adapt the Exodus for the theater and twist the Sybilline oracles to serve apostolic ends.

The book of Wisdom was intended not only to defend but also to illustrate the tradition of Israel; in its pages not even pagans would find anything to wound them. The Jews had forgotten the language of Scripture, so a translation was begun, probably under Ptolemy II Philadelphus (285-246). Although a certain churlish rabbi claimed that "darkness then

[3] L. Bouyer, *The Meaning of Sacred Scripture* (Notre Dame, Ind.: 1958), p. 248. Appendix A, pp. 242-249, is excellent; it deals with the Jewish tradition and goes beyond the inspired writings and concentrates on the apocryphal or rabbinic literature.

covered the earth for three years," his disagreeable conservatism and crabbed humor had no influence. Thus the charism of inspiration was bestowed upon Judaeo-Hellenists and the word of God was expressed in the language of Plato.[4]

Every now and then it is pleasant to discover a beautiful song of one of the *'anawim* in our Greek Bible. In Isaiah 25:1-5 the translator finally decided to handle the original Hebrew freely, and as a result a new poem appeared in which we catch a vivid proof of the permanence of the diaspora ideal of the *'anawim:*[5]

> O Lord, you are my God. I will exalt you, and give glory to your name: for you have done wonderful things, your designs of old, faithful. Amen! Lord! For you have reduced the city to a heap, the strong city to ruin, the house of strangers: to be no city and to be no more built up for ever. Therefore shall a strong people praise you: the city of mighty nations shall fear you. Because you have been a strength to the poor, a strength to the needy in his distress, a refuge from the whirlwind, a shadow from the heat. For the blast of the mighty is like a whirlwind beating against a wall. You will bring down the tumult of strangers, as heat in thirst: and as with heat under a burning cloud, you shall make the branch of the mighty to wither away.[6]

[4] For the content of this paragraph, see Lagrange, *Le Judaïsme avant Jésus-Christ* (Paris: 1931), pp. 480-541.

[5] A passage like this is enough to raise the question of the inspiration of the Septuagint. This problem, as is well known, was reexamined by P. Benoît, O.P. ("La Septante est-elle inspirée?", *Festschrift für Max Meinertz* [Münster: 1951], pp. 1-9), and P. Auvray ("Comment se pose le problème de l'inspiration des Septante," *Revue Biblique*, 1952, pp. 321-336). The latter author favors the idea of the inspiration of the Septuagint as a whole: "If this position were generally adopted, it would not fail to affect the attitude of modern exegetes. First of all, in regard to their attitude to Alexandrian Judaism, which would become more important and would be considered an essential stage in the history of revelation, a link between post-exilic Palestinian orthodoxy and the New Testament world. But above all, in regard to the Alexandrine version, which would cease to be a mere instrument of textual criticism, a means of establishing the original text of the Bible, and would be studied for its own sake, as the word of God and source of revelation on the same level as the Hebrew text" (*op. cit.*, p. 333).

[6] Translation made by J. Coste, S.M.

In the descriptions of the end of the world and the triumph of Israel found in the apocalypse (Is. 24–27), the theme of the two cities, so popular in works of this kind,[7] has a place of primacy. What is the city of pride (26:5) and the city of nothingness (24:10)? Lindblom suggests Babylon,[8] which is perhaps too specific. At the late date when this apocalypse was written, the unnamed city is more likely a symbol of evil, just as Sion is a symbol of good. The final gathering together of God's people in Jerusalem will be the vindication of the "poor." The dispersion was for them a violent experience; but even when, humanly speaking, they were not too unhappy (for example, during the Persian period) and continued to use clichés from the exile to describe their condition, they transposed them to signify the spiritual thirst from which they suffered:

> If I forget you, Jerusalem, may my right hand be forgotten! (Ps. 136:5).

These "poor men" knew that they were God's favorites. The book of Baruch, a product of the Alexandrian dispersion and perhaps contemporary with the writings of Ben Sirach, preserves a prayer of confession and confidence that was recited in the synagogues (Bar. 1:15–3:8). There we read:

> Look down upon us, O Lord, from your holy house, and incline your ear and hear us. Open your eyes and behold. For the dead that are in hell, whose spirit is taken away from their bowels, shall not give glory and justice to the Lord. But the soul that is sorrowful for the greatness of evil she has done and goes bowed down and feeble, and the eyes that fail, and the hungry soul gives glory and justice to you the Lord (Bar. 2:16-18).

Here the vocabulary is not technical but the climate of thought is one we know well (Is. 66:1-2[9] and Ezek. 34:16, where

[7] It suffices to cite Apocalypse 11:2, 7; 17:21.
[8] Cited in A. Bentzer, *Introduction to the Old Testament*, II (1948), p. 114.
[9] See p. 34.

Yahweh proclaims His attachment to the weak and trusting sheep of His fold).[10]

Greek canticles inserted in the book of Daniel repeat the same theme. The canticle of the three young men in the burning furnace (Dan. 3:51-90) contains the invitatory (v. 87): "O you holy *(osioi)* and humble of heart *(tapeinos kardia)*, bless the Lord." The canticle of Azariah (3:25-45) contains a prayer (v. 39) which obviously owes its inspiration to Psalm 50:19: "Lord, may we be heard for our contrite heart and humbled spirit *(tapeinomenos)*." Theodotion speaks of "our spirit of humility" *(tapeinoseos)*, and the absolute use of *tapeinos* in this sense should not be forgotten when we listen to the *Magnificat*.

But it is in Palestine itself that we can follow the evolution of the theme of poverty. The recent sensational discoveries at Qumran have revolutionized, as is well known, our knowledge of Judaism in the first and second centuries before Christ. The excavations of 1947, 1949, 1951 and 1952 have slowly disclosed, not far from the Dead Sea, the convent, the rule and the library of a Jewish sect that is more and more frequently recognized as Essenian.[11] This group, facing a danger which must surely have been the Roman war of 66-70 A.D., hid their books, before evacuating, in several recently discovered caves. The newly-found texts raise as many questions as they answer. No complete agreement has been reached as to the dates or even as to the identity of the Qumran sectarians.[12] But the discovery has clarified our understanding of pre-Christian literary trends. Père Lagrange believed that the book of Jubilees, the Testament of the Twelve Patriarchs

[10] On Palestinian soil a rereading of a difficult text introduces an allusion to the "poorest (*'aniyyim*) of the flock" (Zech. 11:7, 11).

[11] A. Dupont-Sommer, *Nouveaux aperçus sur les manuscrits de la mer Morte* (Paris: 1953). (English translation: *The Jewish Sect of Qumran and the Essenes, New Studies on the Dead Sea Scrolls*, London, 1954.)

[12] A good study of various opinions is given by E. Jacob in *État présent des études vétéro-testamentaires* (Montpellier: 1952), pp. 23-43. Jacob is inclined to accept the Essenian hypothesis. Barthelemy *(Revue Biblique*, 1952, p. 205) believes that the documents may reflect successive stages, from the Hasidim, contemporaries of the Maccabean revolt, up to the Essenians.

and the Henoch literature were Essenian in origin.[13] This suggestion is winning supporters. It also seems reasonable that the mysterious Zadokite Damascus Document belonged to the Qumran sect (at Qumran some fragments of the document were discovered). But this reclassification does not affect all the writings of this complex period; the Psalms of Solomon are still attributed to the Pharisees.

For our purpose it suffices to recall that beginning in the second century the infiltrations and encroachments of Hellenism aroused strong sectarian resistance. Their defense of the traditional faith took many forms, depending on the historical situation and the initiative of dominant personalities. The principle of "separation" for the preservation of the Jewish faith was basic as far back as the reforms of Ezra and Nehemiah. In their determination to establish a pure Israel, free from all semi-pagan compromises, they free themselves from the Samaritans and those Jews guilty of contracting mixed marriages. The psalter provides proof of the hatred of these two irreconcilable blocs. As these blocs hardened, they turned into sects, with a solid sociological substructure and instinctive feeling of self-defense.

When Mattathias, the father of the Maccabees, formed bands to resist the edict of Antiochus IV Epiphanius (175-164), there was a compact *(synagoge)* group of Hasidim who came to his rescue. Père Abel compares these "Torah volunteers," whose name means "the Pious," to medieval military orders (1 Mac. 2:42).

This explains the origin of the Pharisees. Their name means "Separatists" and dates from their break with the Hasmoneans under John Hyrcanus (135-104). They were restored to favor under Alexander (76-67). Later they prided themselves that they were the true Israel, uncontaminated by the *'am ha'areṣ*. "Seeing that the Mosaic Law was not able to protect them from every impure contact, they introduced many additional prescriptions so as to widen the hedge separating the Jew from the uncircumcised. The word *Pharisee*

[13] *Le Judaïsme avant Jésus-Christ* (Paris: 1931), pp. 121, 130, 329, 425.

denotes the meticulous care with which they isolated themselves from the common people and their easy-going ways. In their pursuit of the principle of separation, they eventually succeeded in leading a life that distinguished them not only from foreigners but also from all other observers of the Jewish law."[14] They looked on themselves as "companions" (*haberim*).

The Essenes also traced their origin to the Hasidim. But they succeeded in lifting sectarian regimentation to a kind of summit. The *Manual of Discipline* is the rule of "God's Party" (*esah*).[15] Membership was voluntary (*nedabim*). The initiation ceremony was preceded by a postulantship and noviceship. Order was preserved by a code of punishments. Manual work, silence, meals in common, scripture reading, daily bath, communal ownership of goods, reverence for celibacy (at least by certain members) — these were some of the sect's characteristics. In the solitude of Qumran, close to the "motherhouse," they practiced "desert spirituality."

These facts about the three sects are a summary and a simplification. Certain sociologico-religious factors were gradually modified and during this evolution each sect became more sharply defined. The Pharisees described by the evangelists, Paul and Josephus were not necessarily the "Separatists" of early days. Philo and Josephus give us a fairly late picture of the Essenes. It must not be forgotten that the members of "God's Party" also called themselves the "Sons of Zadok." The first Sadducees were evidently not what they were to become in the Gospels. The historian Josephus speaks of these three sects in clearly distinct terms, but in earlier times they seem to have been closely related to one another and the vocabulary of poverty shows this connection.[16]

14 F.-M. Abel, *Histoire de la Palestine depuis la conquête d'Alexandre jusqu'à l'invasion arabe* (1952), I, 220. For the *'am ha'areṣ*, see above p. 18, note 6, chapter I.

15 Dupont-Sommer, *op. cit.*, p. 92, proposes the hypothesis that the Essenes derived their name from *esah*, i.e., they were the people of the Party.

16 See what D. Barthélemy has to say in "Notes en marge de publications récentes sur les manuscrits de Qumran," *Revue Biblique*, 1952, pp. 205, 213-218.

The books of Henoch and the Psalms of Solomon give us the traditional contrast between the *ʿanawim* and the impious. A. Causse, in his alert study of *Les "pauvres" d'Israel,*[17] has made an anthology of texts that can easily be sampled. The original Hebrew text that the Pharisee author ascribed to Solomon during the days of Pompey's invasion of Palestine has not survived. In its pages the old patterns of the psalmists are easily discerned: these *ʿanawim-ʾebyonim* are less wretched than the poor-in-soul, the clients of the heavenly Father:

> Lord, I shall praise your name with gladness, because you are good and merciful, you are the refuge of the poor *(ptochos)*. When I cry to you, do not turn away from me.... In time of tribulation we call upon you for help, and you will not refuse our request, because you are our God! If I hunger, I shall appeal to you, O God, and you will give me something to eat. You feed birds and fish, and to the grass in the steppe you send rain so that it will grow, and provide food for all who live in the desert. When the animals are hungry, they lift their face to you. You will hear them, because who is good and beneficent, if not you? You rejoice the soul of the humble *(tapeinos)* when you open your hand for him in your mercy.[18]

In the Henoch literature the same accents are heard. The many *Magnificat* clichés testify not to any social vindication but rather to a religious indictment of satisfied souls who strive for the clear water of earthly fountains instead of seeking the only Source of all truth. These souls are blinded by their riches; as Jesus would say later, thorns stifle the word of God.

> Woe to you sinners....Woe to you who devour the flower of wheat, who drink the best water from the fountain and in your power crush the *humble* beneath your feet. Woe to you who drink water in every season, for you will suddenly receive your due. You will be consumed and dried up because you have turned away from the Source of life

17 *Les "pauvres" d'Israel (prophètes, psalmistes, messianistes),* Straşbourg-Paris: 1922, pp. 132-172.

18 *Psalms of Solomon,* 5:1, 2, 7, 10-14 in Causse, *op. cit.,* p. 149.

> ....Woe to you rich men, because you have trusted your riches....[19]

The Qumranites, in their turn, claimed the title of "the poor," so dear to Israel's piety. The psalms they composed show us this still powerful theme in a context of persecution to which it owed, so to speak, its strength.

> You have redeemed the soul of *your poor* ....You are my God. You have come to the rescue of the soul of the *humble* and of the *poor* against one who was stronger than he.[20]

The Habakkuk commentary is the work of an exegete of this period who reinterprets the prophecy in terms of the history of the sect; he alludes to a persecution of the "poor" by an impious priest. It does not matter that the experts have failed to explain this allusion, but it is clear that the sect wished, at a definite moment, to make its own a traditional title. There were "poor" in every part of Israel, not only grouped around a "motherhouse." They were called "the simple," the basic qualification of the ideal religious man. This is a classic term in the Septuagint and will reappear in the New Testament.[21] Here is the commentary development of the Habakkuk text:

> For the iniquity of Libanus shall cover you and the ravaging of beasts shall terrify them, because of the blood of men and of the iniquity of the land and of the city and of all that dwell therein (2:17). This saying means the wicked priest, that to him may be paid his recompense, as he recompensed the poor; for Lebanon is the council of the community, and the beasts are the simple ones of Judah, the doers of the law. God will execute judgment upon him and destroy him, as he plotted to destroy the poor. And as for what it says, for the blood of a city and violence to a land, this means the city, that is Jerusalem, in which the wicked priest wrought abominable works and defiled God's sanctuary; and violence to a land, these are the cities of Judah, because he plundered the wealth of the poor.[22]

[19] Book of Henoch, 96:4-6; 94:8.

[20] This is the Lambert translation of Psalm B in *Nouvelle Revue Théologique*, 1952, p. 285. The word "poor" is also found in Psalm C.

[21] R. Eppel, *Le piétisme juif dans les Testaments des Douze Patriarches* (Paris: 1930), p. 152.

[22] M. Burrows, *The Dead Sea Scrolls* (New York: 1956), p. 370.

So far we have remained within the traditional context; the sectarians seem to have continued and made more emphatic the meaning of *'anawim* that had been established in the psalter. But they went further and made something similar to a "vow of poverty"; and "they lived, by principle and profession, a life of piety, humility and poverty." Loeb is wrong when he uses these terms to describe the *'anawim* in the period of the psalmists, but it is correct to apply them to the period now under discussion.[23]

We must point out that some of Loeb's quasi-romantic ideas about taking pleasure in poverty or freely embracing this state[24] (Causse himself in some ways made the same mistake) are anachronistic in an earlier age. Israel felt no more attraction for poverty than it did for virginity until it received the revelation of life beyond the grave. Not by chance were both these practices held in honor by the Essenians, who held firm beliefs about the next world.

Pliny the Elder describes this "solitary people, singular above all others, who lived without women, without love, without money."[25] Dio Chrysostom was later to call them "a happy City." Into this City Philo and Josephus are able to introduce us. The evidence Josephus offers is of special importance because he lived in the midst of these people. He was deeply impressed by what he saw of their practice of poverty and communal ownership.

> Contemning wealth, they admired a life lived in common. No man is richer than another man, because it is a law that each one surrender his fortune to the corporation when he enters the sect. As a result no one suffers the misery of poverty or enjoys the splendor of wealth. All that is owned, is owned in common; each one possesses one single patrimony....

[23] *Op. cit., pp. VII, 21.* Let us add that Loeb, following Graetz, sought to extend the date of the psalter to the Maccabean period.

[24] "He is humble and poor because he so desires...this is the penalty of being a poet," *op. cit.*, p. 7.

[25] *Hist. natur.*, V, 17. The texts on the Essenians were assembled and translated by Lagrange, *Le Judaïsme avant Jésus-Christ* (Paris: 1931), pp. 307-319.

> No one can buy or sell; instead he gives his brother what he needs and receives in return what he requires. There is no question of exchange as each one freely turns and asks for help from whomever he please.[26]

The *Manual of Discipline* confirms all this. The sect is known as the "Community." The Hebrew noun *yahad* has this meaning. Etymologically it denotes "unity" or "order" and is the equivalent of *koinonia.* The same word *yahad,* used as an adverb, "in common" or "together," recurs with characteristic constancy. For those versed in the covenant, the idea of "unity" and "communion" clearly colors the whole of life.[27]

> Because all things will be in common *(beyahad):*
> Truth and virtuous humility *('anawah)*
> devout love and a concern for justice,
> of one for the other in the holy Party
> and, inasmuch as they are sons of the eternal Assembly.
> And in common *(yahad)* they will eat,
> And in common *(yahad)* they will bless,
> And in common *(yahad)* they will deliberate.
> And those who have volunteered *(nedabim)* for his truth will bring their intelligence and strength and possessions to the community of God, in order to purify their intelligence in the truth of the precepts of God, and to regulate their strength according to the perfection of his ways and all their possessions according to the justice of his counsels.

Does this not recall the idyllic texts that praise the first Christian community of Jerusalem:

> And all who believed were together and held all things in common, and would sell their possessions and goods and distribute them among all according as anyone had need ....Now the multitude of the believers were of one heart and one soul, and not one of them said that anything he possessed was his own, but they had all things in common ....Nor was there anyone among them in want. For those who owned lands or houses would sell them and bring the price of what they sold and lay it at the feet of the apostles,

[26] *Jewish War,* II, 8,3-4.
[27] Dupont-Sommer, *op. cit.,* p. 93.

and distribution was made to each, according as any one had need (Acts 2:45; 4:32, 34-35).

This fraternal and joyous climate was related to the practice of poverty. It recalls the first Franciscan experiences, or Proudhon's phrase, "poverty, the principle of our happiness." The old Pythagorean and Plotinian dream had been transplanted and was flourishing in the religious and typically Jewish soil of the *'anawim and 'ebyonim.*[28] The Jerusalem Church needed only to imitate this pattern of life in common.[29]

It has been observed that the *Manual of Discipline* never refers to its members as "the poor." Yet no one can deny that the word *'anawah,* rich with the acquired meaning of centuries, was dear to them and that *'ebyon* seems to be a favorite in other Qumran documents. Under these circumstances we venture a hypothesis.

When the Christian Church was born in Jerusalem, there grew the realization that its members constituted the true Israel. Naturally they began to use sacred words long connected with the covenant. This was the same vocabulary that Jewish sectarians as well as the "pious" men of the psalms had also claimed as their own.

The Church of Christ continued this trend, or rather the first Christians integrated themselves within it. Canon Cerfaux's thought-provoking pages describing this crossroad in the history of God's people are well known: in Jerusalem the terms "the holy ones" and "the elect" became Christian.[30] We suggest that "the poor," with all the religious overtones that this word eventually acquired, should also be added to his list.

When St. Paul spoke of the collection made in the pagan-Christian churches for the mother-church, he spoke of "a ser-

[28] L. Cerfaux, "La première communauté chrétienne à Jérusalem," *Eph. Theol. Lovan.,* studied the literary influence of the Pythagorean on the account of Acts (Jamblique, *Vita Pyth.,* 167-168; Plato, *Republ.,* V, 462).

[29] The "Ebionites" represent a Judaeo-Christian sect that was soon to be dispersed. We will not speak of it here.

[30] L. Cerfaux, *The Church in the Theology of St. Paul* (New York: Herder and Herder, 1960).

vice made on behalf of the saints" (*hoi hagioi*—2 Cor. 9:1). The Old Testament provides the foundation for a parallel that may be detected in Galatians 2:10, where reference is made to the beneficiaries of this collection, "the poor" (*hoi ptochoi*). Is it temerarious to think that this term also denotes the Church of Jerusalem?

Here our long investigation of the Church of "the poor" comes to an end. We have moved from Zephaniah to St. Paul. The vocabulary of poverty, which at first had a merely sociological significance, in the course of centuries became charged with spiritual values of high intensity. Eventually it was realized that these spiritual values could be preserved only if the material conditions of poverty were reinvented; this is the meaning of the "vow" that took shape in the desert of Judah. True spiritual poverty can never exist without material poverty. Is this not the lesson that the Qumranites teach at the threshold of the New Testament?

We have also seen that the ideal of the *'anawah* was understood by a constantly decreasing number; this is another instance of the law that God acts through minorities and élites. To such groups as the psalmists, the predecessors of the "poor" whom Luke introduces in the first chapters of both his Gospel and his Acts, God entrusts an essential religious message. This seems to be the dialectic of the Old Testament where all this can be seen, or rather the whole divine pedagogy, patiently working out the divine plan. But when Christ proclaims the beatitude of the *'anawim*, this message will be seen in all its splendor and will be manifest to the whole world.

CHAPTER 5

The Messiah of the 'anawim

This was the way, according to the history we have traced, that the Church of the poor became "the people of God," the praying, waiting, always faithful Israel. Their inner attitude was spiritual and eschatological. There was tension in their advance towards God. These were the people Yahweh loved, and when His hour sounded, they were the messianic people. Their great hopes became a reality. From generation to generation, from the message proclaimed by Zephaniah to the prayers recited by the Qumranites, from the songs of the Second-Isaiah to the silence of Nazareth, this people grew and waited for the moment of their elevation. The hour depended on God alone, but the dynamism of faith activated the preparations, overcame disappointments, preserved tensions. The "poor" sing the praise of the era of deliverance before its arrival, sure that in it there is reserved for them a place of special honor. Their songs, despite accents of impatience and revenge, express the pure hope of those who have risen above what is merely human and have placed all their trust in God.

> The needy and the poor (*'aniyyim, ptochoi*) seek for waters, and there are none:[1] their tongue has been dry with thirst. I Yahweh will hear them, I the God of Israel will not forsake them (Is. 41:17).

[1] The words "and the *'ebyonim*" are omitted as superfluous in this verse. For the theme of spiritual thirst, see Isaiah 32:6; 44:3; 55:1ff.

> And the meek (*'anawim, ptochoi*) shall increase their joy in Yahweh...(Is. 29:19).
>
> The foot shall tread it down: the feet of the poor (*'aniyyim, praeis*), the steps of the needy (*dallim, tapeinoi*)...(Is. 26:6).
>
> The poor people (*ptochos*) will bless you...(Is. 25:3 Greek).

These texts show the centrality of thoughts about poverty and humility in postexilic faith. Moreover, since these references are found in the most messianic of all Old Testament books, the prophecies of Isaiah, they afford an insight into the future elevation of the "poor" in the kingdom that is to come.

This was the dream that the exiles cherished when they prepared to leave Babylon and return to their own land.[2] The whole world and the heavens above were invited to share their joy

> because Yahweh has comforted his people and will have mercy on his poor ones (*'aniyyim*) — Is. 49:13.

Yahweh was about to manifest His power and lead His people in a new exodus. Across the Syrian desert, by the most direct route, Israel returned to Sion. The victories of Cyrus, and especially the fall of Babylon, freed God's people, whom He led in majestic cortege (Is. 52:11-12). At His passage the desert was transformed (Is. 40:3-5; 41:17-19; 43:19-20),

[2] There is a theory advanced by critical scholars that Isaiah 40—55 was written between 546 to 539 and was addressed to this group. This reading is a hypothesis that Canon Coppens, professor of the University of Louvain, admits is "at the least a probable opinion" (*Histoire critique des Livres de l'Ancien Testament*, 1942, p. 192). According to a 1908 decree of the Biblical Commission, this hypothesis was then not based on fully convincing solid arguments, but it would seem that the work of Catholic exegetes during the past fifty years has increased the weight of these arguments. "A constantly increasing number of Catholic authors believe it extremely probable that the Book of Consolation is the work of a disciple of Isaiah who lived during the exile" (Auvray and Steinmann, *Isaïe, La Bible de Jérusalem*, 1951, p. 14). Above all, see A. Feuillet, "Isaïe," *Supplement au Dictionnaire de la Bible*, Vol. IV, col. 690ff. Kissane, an Irish exegete, holding a conservative position, proposes a hypothesis that may rally traditionalists and partisans of the Second-Isaiah. He suggests that an anonymous prophet, well versed in the doctrine of Isaiah, edited his master's work at the end of the exile and adopted it for his contemporaries in the land of Babylon (*The Book of Isaiah*, Dublin: 1943).

> because I have given waters in the wilderness, rivers in the desert, to give drink to my people, to my chosen.

The Israelites understood, as never before, the importance of their role in the history of the world. The meaning of the divine interventions was now clear; their obligation to be witnesses and mediators was equally plain. The return to their own country was a message for the nations and the beginning of their own conversion (Is. 40:5; 42:10; 45:14; 52:10; 54:5):

> Only in you is God; and there is no God besides you. Verily you are a hidden God, the God of Israel, the Savior.

Let us not forget that the Israel to which these lines refer is defined in religious terms: the remnant (Is. 41:14; 46:3), the poor of Yahweh (Is. 49:13), His redeemed (Is. 51:11), His disciples (Is. 54:13), His servants (Is. 44:1; 54:17), those who hope in Him (Is. 40:31), those who keep the law in their hearts (Is. 51:7), the "race" of Israel-Jacob (Is. 44:3). The word "race" *(zeraʿ)* is invested with a new, religious meaning. Throughout these poems, Israel is often called "Servant" (Is. 41:8-9; 42:19; 43:10; 44:1-2, 21).

So we see that the resonances of this word have changed for the fourth time.[3] However, the innermost meaning of this magnificent symphony is in no sense diminished: salvation will come to Israel, through Israel, and as a result of Israel's worldwide expansion. The concept is now purified of all external spectacular elements and consists of acts of humble preaching and the acceptance of redemptive death. Salvation, so long hoped for, will come, but God will realize His plan through the gifts and sufferings of a mysterious person.

[3] The four passages are Isaiah 42:1-4 (solemn investiture oracle); 49:1-6 (description of vocation); 50:4-9 (a confession similar to those found in Jeremiah); 52:13—53:12 (a collective royal lament preceded and followed by an oracle of Yahweh). For various exegetical theories, van der Ploeg, *Les Chants du Serviteur de Yahvé dans la seconde partie du livre d'Isaïe,* (Paris: 1936); H. H. Rowley, *The Servant of the Lord and Other Essays on the Old Testament* (London: 1952); above all, C. R. North, *The Suffering Servant in Deutero-Isaiah* (Oxford: 1948). See, too, *Isaiah,* 40—55 (London: 1952). Our interpretation has been drawn in part from North's book.

How explain this change in perspective? Merely as a hypothesis we propose that the prophet met with failure in his life. The return from exile started as early as 538. It was quiet and only a few Israelites were involved. Some hundred years later, Ezra was the leader of an important caravan (Ezra 8). Meanwhile the announcement of the return had become a theme of postexilic literature (Is. 57:19; Haggai 2:7-8; Zech. 8:7; 10:10; Ps. 68:36). Yet there was no sign of the conversion of the nations, although both Haggai (2:22) and Zechariah (2:15) had expected it.

All these incidents had seemed part of God's plan, according to the prophet of the exile. So true were they that he took them just as they had always been understood but in a new perspective. This time God's plan would succeed (Is. 53:10); it would include the regrouping of Israel and the conversion of the pagans; but it would be the achievement of a Man of tomorrow, not the work of Cyrus (Is. 44:28). This Israelite of the future would resemble Moses and (most especially) Jeremiah. The efficacy of his martyrdom was expressed in liturgical terms (just as the first Christians had described the death of Jesus). Delicate allusions, borrowed from royal messianism (Is. 42:1; 53:12), left no doubt that he was a figure of the Messiah.

Thus the Second-Isaiah, enlightened by revelation, deepened earlier perspectives. We may suppose that he did this surrounded by disciples to whom he entrusted what we might call his last will and testament. This they later placed among his poetry after adding some literary touches of their own. The four songs of the Suffering Servant were thus preserved and they contain what the exegete North has called "the living heart of his message."

What is the exact profile of this eschatological personage? With what elements, fashioned in the present and projected into the future, did the inspired author construct him? We might answer that the Servant alone will incarnate and recapitulate the "ideal Israel" theology formulated in exile times:

> And he said to me: You are my servant Israel, for in you will I glory (Is. 49:3).

If it is foolish to want to get rid of a text[4] that contains so precious an indication, it is equally wrong to adopt a collective interpretation, as if in this sentence "Israel (was) poetically personified...and the prophet was summing up in the idea of Servant, Israel's providential mission as Yahweh's missionary in the world and mankind's scapegoat" (Loisy). In fact, the Servant is not to be identified simply with a fervent Israel whom it is his vocation to resemble (Is. 49:6).

Yet his connection with Israel is true and deep. After the exile the prophets did not fail to continue to admonish the people as they had done before. These clear-thinking mentors and spiritual leaders of the theocracy had become the structuring element of a people now without king and clergy. They were, so to speak, their only reference, their only bond. This explains the new emphasis on messianism: the Messiah-Prophet replaces the Messiah-King.

Two major representatives were selected from all these men sent by God: Jeremiah, whose significance was more and more understood during the exile, and Moses, the super-prophet of Numbers 12:6-8. The Servant resembled them both, but on an entirely different plane. His ministry, like theirs, was one of intercession (Is. 53:12; cf. Jer. 7:16; 11:14; 15:1; 37:3; Ex. 32:32). He, too, would be dedicated to the preaching of the divine "Word" and "Torah" (Is. 42:4). The struggle against sin would be central in his life (Is. 53) as it had been in theirs (e.g., Jer. 6:27-30). In his ministry he would also know opposition (Is. 49:4; 50:4-9). The contradictions he met were similar to those experienced by Jeremiah.

It would be easy to discover further resemblances: the vocation *ab utero* (Is. 49:1; Jer. 1:5), the habitual dialogue with God (Is. 49:1-6), the willingness to sacrifice everything in Yahweh's service, even to die a martyr's death (Jer. 26). But, Jeremiah would want to add, when the Servant would come he would surpass him in every way: his task would be clearly universal, his response to Yahweh more absolute, his preoccu-

4 "It would greatly simplify the whole problem if we could, in all honesty, eliminate Israel" — C. R. North, *op. cit.*, p. 119.

pation with sin more central, and the redemptive gift of his person would be unique.

Twice the Servant is described in terms of poverty (Is. 53:4, 7). As we shall see, the second reference introduces us to the spiritual climate of an *'anawah:*

> The ideal of piety that is proposed is new. It is the ideal of a divine confidence flowering in resignation and willingly accepted pain. This ideal plainly owes much to the teaching of the prophets but it has insights no prophet ever reached and which even a Jeremiah understood only in his best moments. Those most perceptive of the psalmists, in later years, alone could understand and accept this with all the ardor of their love. A day would come when the greatest of all the prophets would appear and freely and humbly submit to the most ignominious of all deaths. Full understanding would be possible only when his disciples proclaimed his resurrection and reminded men of all that had been written about the dying and risen Servant of Yahweh.[5]

FOURTH SONG OF THE SERVANT (Is. 52:13—53:12)[6]

(Oracle of Yahweh)

Behold, my servant shall understand;
    he shall be exalted and extolled
    and shall be exceedingly high.
As many have been astonished at you,
    so shall his visage be inglorious among men
    and his form among the sons of men.
He shall sprinkle many nations;
    kings shall shut their mouth at him.
For they to whom it was not told of him have seen:
    and they that heard not have beheld.

[5] Gunkel, *Die Propheten* (Göttingen: 1917), p. 103.
[6] Cf. Kissane's reading for 53.

(Lamentation of the kings of the earth)

Who has believed our report?
and to whom is the arm of the Lord revealed?
He shall grow up as a tender plant before him,
and as a root out of a thirsty ground.
There is no beauty in him, nor comeliness;
we have seen him, and there was no sightliness,
that we should be desirous of him:
despised and the most abject of men,
a man of sorrows and acquainted with infirmity,
and his look was as it were hidden and despised,
whereupon we esteemed him not.
Surely he has borne our infirmities and carried our sorrows,
and we have thought him as it were a leper,
and as one struck by God and afflicted.
But he was wounded for our iniquities,
he was bruised for our sins.
The chastisement of our peace was upon him,
and by his bruises we are healed.
All we like sheep have gone astray,
every one has turned aside into his own way,
and Yahweh has laid on him the iniquity of us all.
He was offered because it was his own will,
and he opened not his mouth.
He shall be led as a sheep to the slaughter
and shall be dumb as a lamb before his shearer,
and he shall not open his mouth.
He was taken away from distress and from judgment.
Who shall declare his generation?
Because he is cut off out of the land of the living:
for the wickedness of my people have I struck him.
He shall give the ungodly for his burial
and the rich for his death,
because he has done no iniquity,
neither was there deceit in his mouth.
Yahweh was pleased to bruise him in infirmity.
If he shall lay down his life for sin,
he shall see a long-lived seed,
and the will of Yahweh shall be prosperous in his hand.

(Oracle of Yahweh)

Because his soul has labored,
he shall see and be filled.

By his knowledge shall this my just servant justify many,
and he shall bear their iniquities.
Therefore will I distribute to him very many,
and he shall divide the spoils of the strong,
because he has delivered his soul unto death
and was reputed with the wicked.
He has borne the sins of many
and has prayed for the transgressors.

Scholars are at present rediscovering and re-evaluating the Suffering Servant motif in Judaism. It is sufficient to name H. Reisenfeld, J. Jeremias, Stamm, Bentzen and Dupont-Sommer. The latter has not hesitated to stress the importance of Psalm 21 in this perspective. There can be no doubt that this psalm was understood in messianic terms long before the Christian era and it is possible to trace this deepening meaning. For many years Israel cherished this strength-giving text. Let us examine briefly four successive readings.

Jeremiah was one of the first Israelites to set down in writing the painful experiences and the failures of a difficult ministry, the moods of elation and discouragement that alternately swept his soul, the soliloquies that at times became a mystical dialogue. Baruch, his faithful secretary, transcribed these "confessions" and added them to the prophet's oracles.[7]

This new and delightfully spontaneous literary form was immensely successful. Postexilic prophets like Isaiah (49:1ff; 50:4ff) and the psalmists (Ps. 50) quickly adopted it. The memoirs of Nehemiah are a proof of its influence. The spiritual canticles in the psalter (Pss. 16, 87, 139) reflect both Jeremiah's spirit and style and were the favorite meditation for many devout souls, especially for the *'anawim*.

The original reading of Psalm 21 must be understood in this light.[8] The author makes his identity very clear, calls himself "a poor man" (*'ani, ptochos* — v. 25), lists all his misfortunes. Sickness is, as it were, the background of his troubles:

[7] See p. 46.

[8] For the translation and for this first reading, see E. Podechard, *Le Psautier, traduction littérale et explication historique* (Lyons: 1949), pp. 102-109.

> I am like water poured out; all my bones are racked. My heart has become like wax melting away within my bosom. My throat is dried up like baked clay, my tongue cleaves to my jaws; to the dust of death you have brought me down (v. 15-16).

Medical references in the Bible are usually vague; broken bones (Ps. 50:10), out-poured blood (Ps. 50:16) are descriptive clichés without diagnostic value. In this way we must understand the poor man when he speaks of his fever, exhaustion and loss of weight. His condition is the result, if we accept St. Jerome's reading of 21:17, of persecution and imprisonment:

> Indeed, many dogs surround me, a pack of evildoers closes in upon me; they have bound my hands and my feet and in the dust of death they have laid me. I can count all my bones. They look on and gloat over me; they divide my garments among them, and for my vesture they cast lots (Ps. 21:17, 16, 18-19).

Baruch makes many references to prisoners in his reports about Jeremiah (37-38). In those days imprisonment did not mean isolation. The prisoner in the following quotation complains that people scoff at him:

> All who see me scoff at me; they mock me with parted lips, they wag their heads (Ps. 21:8).

Did they equate sickness and sin, just as did Job's friends? Or, did they heartlessly take malicious pleasure in the fall of a just man? Their attacks wounded the psalmist, yet his own explosive retaliations were vehement; he railed loudly against all those, jailers or judges, who were, directly or indirectly, responsible for his condition. He multiplied abusive epithets, stigmatizing his enemies as bulls, lions, buffalos, and even dared to call them dogs. Père Lagrange was most flattering when he claimed that he found the psalmist free from "any ill-feeling against his captors; no curses, no bitter complaints crossed his lips."[9]

[9] "Notes sur le messianisme dans les Psaumes," *Revue Biblique*, 1905, p. 51.

Humanly speaking, he was without hope. God was deaf to his pleas:

> My God, my God, why have you forsaken me? (v. 1).

God's silence was unexpected. Making his own a Jeremaic theme (Jer. 1:4; cf. Is. 49:1; Ps. 138:15ff), the psalmist affirmed his belief in God's nearness. This meant everything to him:

> You have been my guide since I was first formed, my security at my mother's breast. To you I was committed at birth, from my mother's womb you are my God. Be not far from me (Ps. 21:10-12).

These statements are not misleading — it is obvious that he expected all things from God whom he loved (v. 9). This quality of soul, this habitual, trustful recourse to God, this attitude of a "client" defines spiritual poverty, for it is born, or at least deepened, in failure and suffering.

If the *'ani* took a long time to describe his trial, it was probably due to the fact that it was almost at an end. Suddenly he had an intuition of the happiness ahead. It was customary for men freed from prison, convalescents after an illness, travelers who had crossed the desert, sailors at the close of a safe sea journey (Ps. 106) to offer a thanksgiving sacrifice in the temple. Psalm 117 gives us, as it were, the libretto of this *shelem,* a paraliturgical ceremony, in which these people fulfilled their vows.

They expressed their joy in canticles. The temple choirs sang their usual invitatories (v. 24); the joy of the brethren added to the musical gladness. The *'anawim* took part in the celebration (v. 27); these pious men are described in terms similar to those noted in Psalm 33: "they fear Yahweh" (v. 26) and "they seek him" (v. 27). They are part of a great postexilic religious movement, the chosen "remnant" fashioned by the prophets. On such an occasion they were in the temple rejoicing in Yahweh's presence, and took part in the sacred repast that completed the sacrifice. At the close the psalmist recalled the wishes customary when men sat down to eat:

> The lowly (*ʿanawim*) shall eat their fill; they who seek Yahweh shall praise him: "May your hearts be ever merry!" (v. 27).

This was an original composition. Because of its beauty it was retained in one of the official Temple collections. This explains the title placed at the beginning of the psalm, indicating its nature and manner of presentation.

It was correctly called a psalm and was soon to enter upon the second stage of its use, which may well be described as the liturgical phase. It was incorporated in the newly composed liturgical thanksgivings. Most of these hymns were nondescript (cf. Pss. 5, 6) but the concrete details were soon to be blurred in the new climate. We can repeat with Msgr. Garrone, who asked in reference to the singing of old Hebrew psalms in our churches: "Can we deny that these words possess a religious quality, a power of recollection that, up to a point, is completely independent of the intellectual content of the text?"[10]

It was here that the psalm acquired its most important meaning, i.e., its messianic meaning. One day, perhaps towards the end of the fourth century, an important addition polarized the facts of the psalm and oriented them towards the future. Verses 28-32 contain a wonderful extension of perspective, a picture of God's kingdom, of which there are few in the Bible and which point to a later date of composition. Connected with what went before, the vision deals with Yahweh's ecumenical reign — in the style of the so-called kingdom psalms (e.g., Ps. 97), which orchestrate the statements in Isaiah 52:8 — then with the truths about those who have risen from the dead and who will people the new kingdom,[11] and lastly with the generation of the age to come. Thus from every point of the compass all mankind will praise the Lord in a concert in which those who have died in the past will unite with those who will live in the future.

[10] *Psaumes et prières* (Toulouse: 1952), p. 12.

[11] The doctrine of the resurrection is stated in the apocalypses (Dan. 12 and Is. 26) and in Maccabees; all are late texts.

> All the ends of the earth shall remember and turn to the Lord; all the families of the nations shall bow down before him. For dominion is Yahweh's, and he rules the nations. To him alone shall bow down all who sleep in the earth; before him shall bend all who go down into the dust. And to him my soul shall live; my descendants shall serve him. Let the coming generation be told of the Lord that they may proclaim to a people yet to be born the justice he has shown (Ps. 21:28-32).

How is such a startling combination possible? It is obviously the work of a community of singers who have found the ideal of the *'anawim* attractive and are aware of the messianic longing expressed in the fourth song of the Suffering Servant (Is. 52:13–53:12). The new revelation of the Messiah introduced ideas of suffering, of redemptive sacrifice and the success of the divine plan. The Isaian rhythm moved from failure to success, as does the rhythm of our psalm. The Poor Man of the psalm, like the Servant in Isaiah, became a great eschatologic figure through the extraordinary elevation of which he is the occasion.

It is true that in Isaiah, the Servant, by his sufferings, brings about the success of God's plan and it must be admitted that this relation is not stressed in the psalm. Must we conclude that the only really significant characteristic of Isaiah 53 is missing in our psalm?[12] To do so would be to forget the artificial nature of the addition that made the psalm messianic.[13] The process was not perfect, but it seems to have been sufficiently clear to men who were less "logical" than we and who had made the hopes instilled by Isaiah 53 central in their thinking.

The third reading of Psalm 21 may be made this way: the Poor Man of the last days will experience suffering but he will be delivered by God, and this deliverance will coincide

[12] Lagrange, *op. cit.*, p. 52.

[13] According to H. Schmidt *(Die Psalmen,* Tübingen: 1943), two antiphons (22b: "thou hast heard me"; 32c: "behold what he has done"), accent the (artificial) unity of the thanksgiving section of the psalm (vv. 23-32). In this way the eschatologic "Poor Man" is placed in the center of the kingdom of God.

with the messianic era, of which he will be the center. All this is sung in the prophetic past tense, as is customary in messianic compositions; thus the impression is given that the event has already taken place.

The fourth reading is Christologic and is a more sharply focused version of the third. We shall make a distinction between the reading of Christ Himself and that of the first generation of Christians.

From the temptation in the desert to the three statements Christ made on His way to Jerusalem (Matthew 16:21ff; 17:22-23; 20:17-19), Jesus plainly elected a humble and suffering messianism, fulfilling the expectations of the two Old Testament witnesses we have cited. Jesus incorporated some of these prophetic fragments in His own filial prayer. It is most significant that His last words on the Cross were precisely the opening words of Psalm 21:

> My God, my God, why have you forsaken me?[14]

To quote the opening words of a book or a passage was, for a Jew, to recall the whole meaning of the document. This too-little noted psychology of citation is verified, for example, in Jeremiah 33:11, where the first words of Psalm 117 suffice to recall the spirit of the festivities of the return from exile. Therefore we may say that Jesus made Psalm 21 His own according to the third reading. On His lips this was the cry of the Messiah confidently affirming that He would complete His work. "This was not a cry of revolt or despair but the prayer of a just man who knew in the midst of His sufferings that the God of all holiness would protect Him until death."[15]

[14] Cited in Aramaic by Matthew and Mark, v. 19 becomes "My strength, my strength, why hast thou abandoned me?" Luke and John omit the words, but perhaps they substituted something equivalent (Luke 23:46: an explicit word of confidence from Psalm 30:6; John 19:30: Christ's statement that He had completed His messianic work).

[15] Loisy, *Les Évangiles synoptiques*, II, p. 685, approved by Lagrange, *Évangile selon saint Marc* (Paris: 1920), p. 405. For the same opinion see Huby, *Évangile selon saint Matthieu* (Paris: 1924), p. 466; Buzy, *La Sainte Bible* of Pirot-Clamer, IX, pp. 375-466. "It is remarkable that the development of exegesis has led to a return to the traditional ideas of the Fathers and has corrected many exaggerated statements made about the *Deus meus*" — L. Mahieu, "L'abandon du Christ sur la Croix," *Mélanges de Science religieuse* (Lille: 1945), p. 239.

"Nor did the Jews consider it to be an expression of despair... far from anything like impiety or rebellion, it is consonant with Old Testament piety and therefore is a manifestation of communion with God."[16] This is its primary meaning. To call it "a cry of despair" (Goguel) or to make it the point of departure for a somber theory of dereliction, as many preachers have done, is to misinterpret it completely.[17]

The Christian community also read the psalm in the light of the separate scenes of the Passion; their meditation helped them to understand the scandal of the Cross. The horrible torture inflicted on the Messiah was the fulfillment of the divine will as laid down in the Old Testament. In its prophetic oracles they found the justification of the crucifixion. "Testimonies"[18] were collected, meticulous lists compiled by men who were filled with a great personal love for our Savior, Jesus Christ.

This was not all. Admittedly, more details about the Passion were known than were recorded in our canonical Gospels. A choice had to be made. So incidents fulfilling Old Testament prophecies were selected in order to strengthen men's faith. Scenes of Christ suffering were included because of references in our psalms (Matthew 27:39, 43 and Ps. 21:8-9). This also explains the division of garments (John 19:24; Matthew 27:35 and Ps. 21:19). This last fact is particularly important and has some apologetic significance. When Goguel declared[19] that prophecy begot the Gospel account, he misunderstood the meaning of a poetic text where the second line parallels and merely repeats the thought of the first:

> They divided my garments among them and for my vesture they cast lots (Ps. 21:19).

[16] M. Dibelius, "La signification religieuse des récits évangéliques de la Passion," *Revue d'Histoire et de Philosophie Religieuse*, 1933, p. 35.

[17] L. Mahieu (*op. cit.*, pp. 209-242) gives some of these exaggerated statements which began with the Protestants in the sixteenth century.

[18] This literature is studied in R. Harris, *Testimonies* (2 vols., 1916, 1920). Lists of messianic texts were prepared for Christian missionaries. It is necessary to study them in order to understand the pre-history of our New Testament texts. See C. H. Dodd, *According to the Scriptures* (London: 1952), pp. 28-60.

[19] In his *Vie de Jésus* (Paris: 1932), p. 521.

From this verse it would never have been possible to construct the scene in the fourth Gospel, but the old text acquired a rich new meaning on Calvary and pointed to a pre-established harmony.

We have moved into the New Testament. There we will find another text with which we wish to close this chapter. In the haphazard collection of messianic prophecies in the second part of Zechariah there is a hymn of welcome to the Messiah-King on His entrance into His city.[20] As a reaction against the elaborate panoply of historic kings (Jer. 17:25; 12:4), He is given the age-old mount of desert tribal leaders (Gen. 49:11; Judg. 5:10; 10:4; 12:14). This archaicism is not the only surprising statement in this passage: the Hebrew text presents the Messiah as one who has been "saved," and the Greek text refers to Him as the "savior"; both stress the fact that He has unified Israel and proclaimed universal peace. Most unexpected of all is the use of the title we now know so well, *ʻani-praüs.*[21]

> Rejoice greatly, O daughter of Sion, shout for joy, O daughter of Jerusalem: Behold your King will come to you, the just and savior. He is poor and riding upon an ass and upon a colt, the foal of an ass. And I will destroy the chariot out of Ephraim and the horse out of Jerusalem: and the bow for war shall be broken. And he shall speak peace to the Gentiles, and his power shall be from sea to sea, and from the rivers even to the end of the earth.

[20] Zech. 9–14. We date these chapters from the close of the fourth century. See Haggai, Zechariah, Malachi in *La Bible de Jérusalem*, 1948, p. 23.

[21] Because of the Greek *praüs*, H. Junker *(Die Zwölf Kleinen Propheten* [Bonn: 1938], II, 162) wished to restore *ʻanaw* instead of *ʻani.* This is entirely unnecessary (see Zeph. 3:12). F. Horst *(Die Zwölf Kleinen Propheten* [Tübingen: 1938], p. 238) was shocked to find *ʻani* here and he decided that it was a later addition to what he believed, with Von Kuenen, Baudissin and Steuernagel (p. 207), was a pre-exilic text. But even with this theory, some explanation must be given for the addition of *ʻani* and some attempt must be made to enter into the mind of a scribe who would propose such a rereading of the text.

To the Messiah, therefore, belongs the title that Zephaniah (3:12) attributed to the people of the future and that post-exilic men had applied to David.[22] The influence of Second-Isaiah seems likely. R. Kittel says: "The ideal of humility became an integral part of the messianic figure after Isaiah 40ff"[23]; and K. Elliger, considering the neighboring title of the "just," asks if it is not connected with the Servant of Isaiah 53.[24]

An attempt has been made to clarify the text from Zechariah with the help of some comparisons. As early as the eighth century B.C., *'ani,* it is alleged, was an honorific title according to the inscription of Zakir. A stele records the dangers that were averted by the prayer of the Aramean king of Hamath on the Orontes to the Baal of heaven, when seven kings threatened him. The inscription opens with the words: *'ish 'ani 'ani,* "I am a humble man."[25] According to the context this must refer to his attitude before the god.[26]

If this interpretation of the text is correct, we find here a perfect parallel with the biblical use of *'ani.* Yet this does not prove dependence.

22 See p. 60.

23 *Geschichte des Volkes Israel* (Stuttgart: 1929), III, 692, 245.

24 *Das Buch der Zwölf Kleinen Propheten* (Göttingen: 1950), II, 140.

25 H. Gressmann, *Altorientalische Texte zum Alten Testament* (2nd ed.; Berlin: 1926), p. 443, gives this translation in the German: "I am a man of 'Ana(?)," a city on the Euphrates. The French translation is found in A. Dupont-Sommer, *Les Araméens* (Paris: 1951), pp. 46-47. This author comments: "If he says that he is 'a humble man,' it is not only to exalt the all-powerful help of his God: it is also an allusion to his previous state. "Étude de Sachsse" in *Festschrift E. Sellin,* 1927, pp. 105-110 (*'Ani als Ehrenbezeichnung in inschriftlicher Beleuchtung*) makes the connection with Zechariah 9:9 and Numbers 12:3.

26 Compare the style of royal Neo-Babylonian inscriptions: "Nebuchadnezzar, King of Babylon, the humble, in submissive prayer stands in fear and trembling before the Lord of lords"; cited in Gressmann, *op. cit.,* p. 366.

CHAPTER 6

Mary and Her Song of Poverty

"Because the Blessed Virgin occupies so important a place in the New Law, the faithful take it for granted that in the Old Testament they will find predictions or at least prefigurations of her coming, her virtues and her mission."[1] Let us say at once that these expectations are fulfilled, provided that the Marian orientation of the old economy is seen in proper perspective. Yet, if we examine the countless biblical figures that liturgical piety has connected with our Lady, from Noah's rainbow to the desert propitiatory, from Gideon's fleece to Ezekiel's closed door; and if we hail as her forerunners women who have played important roles in sacred history from Eve to Judith; and if we apply to her the texts on Wisdom personified that we read in Proverbs 8 and Sirach 24; and even if we recognize the Marian prophecy in the literal sense of Isaiah 7:14 and Micah 5:2,[2] we have still failed to consider Mary's most significant and most profound portrait.

In a study that once aroused some interest, Dom Charlier proposed the problem "typology or evolution," pointing out that the first must in some way be integrated in the second.[3] He asked that a study be made of Old Testament faith from

[1] A. Robert, "La Sainte Vierge dans l'Ancien Testament," *Maria, études sur la Sainte Vierge*, (Paris: 1949), I, 23.

[2] We are summarizing A. Robert's excellent work cited above, pp. 23-39.

[3] "Typologie ou évolution. Problèmes d'exégèse spirituelle," *Esprit et Vie*, 1949, pp. 578-597.

within in order to establish its deep, living and objective continuity. Against this background, "figures" would stand out sharply and serve as landmarks along the spiritual journey.

In regard to our present question, we should ask ourselves what is Mary's relation to Israel, and we must answer that she is its perfect consummation. The sociological form of the Israelite community changed many times: first, there was a confederation of tribes, assembled about a sanctuary (the so-called amphictyony); then, the kingdom, centralized in a capital and a dynasty; lastly, an ecclesial society focused on the Temple. During the postexilic period, qualitative and dynamic members, selected by the prophets, formed the "remnant" who alone deserved to be called the "people of Yahweh." God was watching over this small band, purifying and preparing them for the coming of the Day:

> And they shall be in all the earth, says Yahweh; two parts in it shall be scattered and shall perish, but the third part shall be left therein. And I will bring the third part through the fire and will refine them as silver is refined, and I will try them as gold is tried. They shall call on my name, and I will hear them. I will say: You are my people. And they shall say: Yahweh is my God (Zech. 13:8-9).

As a matter of fact this people, always being fashioned through the centuries, was composed of *'anawim:*

> For Yahweh loves *his people,* and he adorns the lowly (*'anawim*) with victory (Ps. 149:4).

We can listen to the prayers and the aspirations that these anonymous devout souls offered to God. One day all that they stand for will be concentrated in Mary, the true link connecting the Old Law and the New. Mary will be the momentary echo of a line of praying men and women. She will draw into her soul all the power of their welcome for the God who comes. She will epitomize the measureless longing that is the spiritual dimension of Israel and which will at last bring forth Christ.[4]

[4] In this perspective the Marian reading of Apocalypse 12:1ff. takes on new interest. We know that the woman who is crowned with

The great symphony of prayer that arose from the Church of the poor was a prelude to the *Magnificat*. "The whole spiritual life...of ancient times reached in Mary its apogee, its point of perfect maturity."[5] And each one of the *'anawim*, each member of the true Israel, prepared for and proclaimed her.

At last on a certain day came the mystery of Nazareth. The Incarnation took place in profound silence, well understood by a devout author of the *Palatine Anthology* who paradoxically contrasted Sinai and the lowly village:

> There were trumpets, lightning flashed and the earth trembled. But when you came down to the womb of a Virgin Your little step made not a sound.[6]

The Galilean hamlet was not mentioned in the Old Testament. It was even asked if anything good could come from such a spot (John 1:46). To this place without a past — like the lowly village *(tapeinon chorion)* which the pagan Porphyry[7] said attracted the attention of the gods — was brought the announcement of messianic joy,[8] because at its center was a silence, a surrender, an emptiness, a longing — this was Mary. Among those who were waiting for the kingdom *(hoi prosdechomenoi*, Luke 2:25-38), she was skilled in listening with "ears of faith" *(akoē pisteos)*, and St. Paul considers this the fundamental religious attitude (Gal. 3:2).

"Blessed is she who has believed" is the compliment Elizabeth paid to the Virgin of the Annunciation. On that day Mary understood, as far as it was humanly possible, the unity of her life; she entered into the mystery of her vocation, she committed herself with the whole strength of her youth to the spiritual adventure that far exceeded her own powers and in which she was but the servant of the Lord.

twelve stars and gives birth to the Messiah symbolizes literally the Church of the Old Testament, then the Judaeo-Christian Church (vv. 6, 14-16), and lastly, simply the Church (v. 17).

5 P. R. Bernard, *Le mystère de Marie* (Paris: 1933), p. 101.

6 I, no. 37.

7 *De abstinentia*, II, 16.

8 The *chaire* of Luke 1:28 was understood by several Greek Fathers to mean: "Rejoice." S. Lyonnet, *Biblica*, 1939, pp. 131-141.

Mary did not refuse the word "Blessed." Her cousin's greeting provided the occasion and, as it were, the theme of the *Magnificat* (Luke 1:46-55). "Everything in it flows from its source," says Père Lagrange. It is more than a fabric woven of Old Testament quotations. In it we hear the woman who has so identified herself with the *'anawim* that, conscious of the newness of the Incarnation, she has become their perfect and living expression.

46 My soul magnifies the Lord
47 and my spirit rejoices in God my Savior;
48 Because he has regarded the lowliness of his handmaid; for behold, henceforth all generations shall call me blessed;
49 Because he who is mighty has done great things for me, and holy is his name:
50 And his mercy is from generation to generation on those who fear him.
51 He has shown might with his arm, he has scattered the proud in the conceit of their heart.
52 He has put down the mighty from their thrones, and has exalted the lowly.
53 He has filled the hungry with good things, and the rich he has sent away empty.
54 He has given help to Israel, his servant, mindful of his mercy —
55 Even as he spoke to our fathers — to Abraham and to his posterity forever.

The first part of the poem (vv. 46-49) is an explosion of happiness and an outpouring of gratitude. This young woman knew that in some hidden way she was at the heart of the history of salvation; all the ages to come will remember her and all the ages passed have prepared formulas of prayer or pride that she can now use. Did not the sterile Hannah, one of the *'anawim,* sing her own *Magnificat* when little Samuel was born?

> My heart has rejoiced in Yahweh, and my horn is exalted in my God; my mouth is enlarged over my enemies, be-

> cause I have joyed in your salvation. There is none holy as the Lord is, for there is no other beside you, and there is none strong like our God (1 Sam. 2:1-2).[9]

To describe the joy of the Messiah's arrival, Mary allowed herself to use the same terms that were used to describe God's most startling works. The ancient "wonders" included: creation (Job 5:9), the miracles of the Exodus (Ex. 3:20; 34:10; Josh. 3:5), the gift of the Law (Ps. 118:18); but Mary is the instrument of "wonders" far more great. We see her lost in admiration before the divine selection of what St. Paul would one day give the consistency of a law: "God chooses the weak things of this world."[10] Mary speaks of her *tapeinosis*, and the word is so central in her poem that it would be surprising if it did not reveal to us her soul. Yet it has troubled translators who fear to make it mean too much. According to L. Marchal, it explains Mary's hidden, obscure situation. R. A. Gauthier thinks it refers to the misery of the human condition. Translators often choose "lowliness" as its equivalent (Joüon, Hilion, Lagrange) or "humility" (Goguel). One edition may elect one translation, the second may prefer the other (Crampon, Osty).

The real problem is to discover exactly what *tapeinosis* meant at this time. The support of the Septuagint is of doubtful value and it is only in Theodotion's version that the word occurs in Daniel 3:39.[11] The evidence of *The Testament of the Twelve Patriarchs*[12] would be precious were it free from all Christian editing. In it Reuben exhorts his descendants to "draw near to Levi in the humility of their hearts *(tapeinosis kardias)*, so that they may receive a blessing from his lips" (Reuben, 6, 10). In the *Testament of Gad* (v. 3) are sentences in which *tapeinosis* is used in an absolute sense:

> Justice drives away hate, humility *(tapeinosis)* kills it, because the just and the humble *(tapeinos)* blush to commit evil.

[9] Hannah's canticle was a later insertion, introduced at a different place and with different formulas in the Hebrew and Greek texts.
[10] 1 Cor. 1:27.
[11] See p. 66.
[12] Greek edition (Oxford: 1908).

Besides, if the meaning of the word were so clearly defined, would Paul have coined the term *tapeinophrosyne* to convey the idea of humility?[13] Consequently it is more prudent to hold that the noun, unlike the adjective *tapeinos* which has long meant "humble,"[14] advanced more slowly toward the meaning of humility.

To understand our Lady's soul, however, it is not necessary to insist on this single word or to isolate it from the sentence. Mary was employing a classic formula that expressed divine solicitude. Samuel's mother, long sterile, had come to the Shiloh temple to ask the Lord to "deign to look upon the humiliation (*'oni, tapeinosis*) of His servant" (1 Sam. 1:11). In the psalmists' petitions and acts of thanksgiving the same formula is used to describe the violent situation, either temporary or permanent, of those who prayed (Ps. 24:18; 30:8). "You saw the affliction (*'oni, tapeinosis*) of our fathers in Egypt," reads a late insertion in Nehemiah (9:9). The expression seems to have had only a vaguely general meaning in liturgical passages, without any allusion to a specific situation. Psalm 118:153 resembles the song of the pariah which we have placed in the appendix. Accordingly, a good translation would be, "See my poverty and deliver me."

Only saints know how to speak humbly of their humility. In the *Magnificat* Mary was able to refer objectively to her humility.[15]

The second part of this "hymn of the poor" brings the blessing of the Incarnation to men who are worthy (vv. 50-53). Anyone familiar with the parallelism and harmonies of the Old Testament can see that "those who fear Yahweh" (v. 50) are His clients, the *'anawim.*[16] They are not the ones the world favors; in fact, their real poverty is the cause of their spiritual

[13] The word is not found in the Septuagint. It does occur in Acts 20:19; Eph. 4:2; Phil. 2:3; Col. 2:18, 23; 3:12; 1 Pet. 5:5. In profane Greek it is used by Josephus (*War* 4:499) and Epictetus (*Interviews* I: 9-10).

[14] See p. 55. Cf. *Lettre d'Aristée* (#263): "God lowers the proud and raises the modest and the humble" (*tapeinoi*).

[15] This paragraph owes much to P. Coste, S.M.

[16] Compare especially Psalm 21:26-27; 33:3-8.

élan. Here three merely human "greatnesses," three "self-sufficiencies" in conflict with God, confront one another: pride (vv. 50-51), power (v. 52), riches (v. 53). But God reverses situations and this is one of the constants of divine Providence that will attain magnificent proportions in messianic days. When Maurras spoke of the "revolutionary venom" of the *Magnificat,* he was placing this value very low. Mary had inherited an old theme that since pagan days defined divine ways.

Marduk was given by his peers in the assembly the power of lowering *(šaphalu)* men or raising them up,[17] and Hesiod sings of Zeus: "With ease he brings down the proud *(arizelos)* and exalts the humble *(adelos)*";[18] and Aesop aptly described the divine interventions that keep the world in order with these words: "He lifts up those who are low and he lowers those who are lifted up."[19] But does this power obey moral laws? Does it not explain the pessimism about the gods that we find in Euripides[20] and that is nowhere to be found in the Bible's moral monotheism?

> Yahweh kills and makes alive, he brings down to hell and brings back again. Yahweh makes poor and makes rich, he humbles and he exalts. He raises up the needy from the dust, and lifts up the poor from the dunghill, that he may sit with princes, and hold the throne of glory. For the poles of the earth are the Lord's, and upon them he has set the world. He will keep the feet of his saints, and the wicked shall be silent in darkness, because no man shall prevail by his own strength (1 Sam. 2:6-9).

These words from Hannah's *Magnificat* are repeated in Mary's *Magnificat.* But the old phrases now have new meaning; biblical tradition and her own "poverty" have transformed them. They now describe the true Christian.

[17] *Enuma elish,* tab. IV, v. 8. See Chapter III, footnote 24.

[18] *Les travaux et les jours,* v. 6. Translated by Mazon.

[19] *Ta hypsela tapeinoi kai ta tapeina anypsoi* (Diogenes Laërtes, *Vit. philos.,* I, 69.)

[20] "Yes, the gods often lower those who are highest and afterwards raise them again" (fragment).

There only remains for Mary to acclaim in the last part of her canticle the salvation accorded to the whole community (vv. 54-55). The Israel to whom she refers is that fervent group whom St. Paul was later to call the Israel of God (Gal. 6:16), and whom the Second-Isaiah in his retrospective history (Is. 41:8) traced back to Abraham, the people whom we now know so well:

> Give praise, O you heavens, and rejoice, O earth. You mountains, give praise with jubilation, because Yahweh has comforted his people, and will have mercy on his poor ones (Is. 49:13).

When Bossuet was about to begin his commentary on the *Magnificat,* he cried out: "What shall I say about this divine canticle? Its simplicity and its majesty are so far beyond my comprehension that they invite me to hold my peace rather than to speak."[21] The celebrated orator knew well that Mary's great soul illumined themes taken from the past and that she drew new meaning from their inmost depths. This spiritual *élan* is instinct in every part of the poem and gives it unity.

The connection between the *Magnificat* and the Beatitudes has not gone unnoticed. "If it were possible to push that far the analysis of the human development (of Jesus), we could say that we can see in Him, as in so many others, something of the influence of His Mother."[22] Yes, it was at Nazareth that the Savior, watching His Mother and listening to her words, loved the *'anawim* whom He would one day declare to be His disciples.

[21] *Élévations sur les mystères,* 14th week, 3rd elevation.
[22] Lagrange, *L'Évangile de Jésus-Christ* (Paris: 1929), p. 51.

CHAPTER 7

Effective Poverty and Spiritual Poverty according to the Gospel

Heir of prophets and sages, Jesus never contradicted what Israel's spiritual guides had taught about the problem of poverty. Far from breaking with tradition, He gave new dimensions to their teaching (Matthew 5:17). Is He not the Light that has come into the world: "God, who at sundry times and in divers manners spoke in times past to the fathers by the prophets, last of all in these days has spoken to us by his Son" (Heb. 1:1-2)? Is He not the living Way we are meant to follow? When we reach Christ, we reach the end of our journey. We have followed Him during the preceding chapters; from Him we receive true directives — if we neglect them we will surely go astray.

Let us first consider the value He attached to effective poverty. The lawgiver of the ancient world had been a realist. He knew that there would always be poor people in the land (Deut. 15:11). On the day before Palm Sunday, Jesus said the same thing (Mark 14:7; Matthew 26:11). Both agreed that the poor must be given every help. But the Gospel explains how this is to be done and the motivation for men's acts of kindness is transfigured. In the Old Testament, mocking the poor was denounced because it displeased God (Prov. 17:5), who cared for them and protected them. Something of this doctrine must have passed into St. James' Epistle, in which certain passages resemble a Jewish catechism: the cries of unpaid workmen reach the Lord's ears (5:4) and the oppression of the poor is an insult to the sacred name (2:7). A commandment specially dear to God is not to be contemned. To look after the poor was one of Job's preoccupations (Job 29:12, 16; 30:25; 31:16, 19); to refuse to succor them is to draw down upon one's self a curse, because God hears their prayers (Sir. 4:6). But such kindness is not yet charity. Causse coined the neologism "charitative." Pity, holy awe, the particularist feeling of the covenant colored the "charitative" practices recommended by the Law and the prophets.

Jesus has taught us to look on the poor as a sacrament of His own presence. In poverty's various countenances we can have a mysterious encounter with Him. Christianity makes these vertical acts habitual. In the description of the last judgment that Jesus gave during Passion week, He revealed the sentence in store for those who practice charity:

> 'Come, blessed of my Father, take possession of the kingdom prepared for you from the foundation of the world; for I was hungry and you gave me to eat; I was thirsty and you gave me to drink; I was a stranger and you took me in; naked and you covered me; sick and you visited me; I was in prison and you came to me.' Then the just will answer him, saying, 'Lord, when did we see you hungry, and feed you; or thirsty, and give you drink? And when did we see you a stranger, and take you in; or naked, and clothe you? Or when did we see you sick, or in prison, and come to you?' And answering the king will say to them, 'Amen I say to you, as long as you did it for one of these, the least of my brethren, you did it for me' (Matthew 25:34-40).

Bossuet says that this text, so important in many ways, establishes the eminent dignity of the poor in the Church. It is their function to keep "the sign of Jesus Christ" living in our midst. He chose poverty, suffering, failure in His Incarnation, in His public life, in His Passion. These "pure scandals, these foolish things. . . God accepts and God wants; and because they prevail in the humanity He personally assumed, they have become the most divine of human realities."[1] This explains Christian devotion to the poor[2] which Bossuet praises in terms that continue to shock: "The Church is truly the city of the poor, the rich inasmuch as they are rich, for we must use these terms correctly; those who belong to the court of the world and bear, so to speak, its stamp, are merely tolerated.... They are foreigners. Only through their service of the poor can they be naturalized...."[3]

"It is easier for a camel[4] to pass through the eye of a needle than for a rich man to enter the kingdom of heaven" (Matthew 19:24). Just as we have seen that the Gospel repeats and deepens an Old Testament idea, namely, Yahweh's preference for the poor, whom He practically identifies as His own people,[5] so here we find that two wisdom themes provide the background. First, wealth isolates its possessors from God and fills them with a sense of their own self-sufficiency; secondly, riches cannot be a final end because they are essentially deceptive.[6] But the Gospel introduces a new note: these relative values are confronted with the kingdom of God, a sharply defined absolute value which is the pearl of great price requiring the surrender of all that we have (Matthew 13:45-46).

Jesus asks us not to be deceived by earthly goods. "The care of this world and the deceitfulness of riches choke the word, and it is made fruitless" (Matthew 13:22). He who aspires to this kingdom fixes his heart where true treasures are to be found, far from the reach of grasping thieves or the destructive power of moths (Luke 12:33-34). The attitude of the rich man to his possessions is sometimes stigmatized in terms of idolatry. Elijah adjured his contemporaries to choose

[1] P. R. Régamey, O.P., *Poverty* (London: 1949), pp. 27-28.

[2] Examples may be found in Régamey, *op. cit.* (cf. "Material Poverty," pp. 17-24); and in Thellier de Poncheville, *L'Évangile dans toute la vie* (Paris: 1930).

[3] "Sur l'éminente dignité des pauvres dans l'Église," *Oeuvres oratoires de Bossuet*, ed. Lebarq, 1890, I, pp. 123, 128.

[4] Or: "for a rope." Bossuet gives both readings in his panegyric of St. Francis of Assisi. In the Armenian version according to St. Cyril of Alexandria *kamelos* is translated by "cord."

[5] See p. 19.

[6] Ps. 48.

Yahweh or Baal and not to waver from side to side (3 Kgs. 18:21). Jesus attacked another idol borrowed from the same pagans of Tyre: "You cannot serve both God and mammon" (Luke 16:13). The wicked rich man drew down upon himself the supreme reproach of having chosen badly: "But Abraham said to him, 'Son, remember that you in your lifetime have received good things" (Luke 16:25). Msgr. Camus observes that this man had given up all else in order to make these possessions his. Is it surprising that if at death he must lose those things that he had made central in his life, he must also forfeit all those other things that he never sought and whose reality he never even admitted?[7] In like manner, the wealthy fool (Luke 12:19-20) was riveted to his riches:

> And I will say to my soul, "Soul, you have many good things laid up for many years; take your ease, eat, drink, be merry." But God said to him, "You fool, this night do they demand your soul of you; and the things that you have provided, whose will they be?"

This man's life was a failure because he had linked it with what perishes.[8]

What Jesus condemned is not wealth as such. He had friends who were well off: the five women who used their own money to assist Him (Luke 8:2-3); Zacchaeus, whose home He visited (Luke 19:1-10); Lazarus, in whose house He received a gift worth three hundred denarii (John 12:5). He was accustomed to social amenities: He attended the wedding feast at Cana (John 2:1-11) and dined with publicans (Matthew 9:10-13). Superficial men contrasted His conduct with that of the ascetic John the Baptist (Matthew 11:18-19). Effortlessly He was able, like the Apostle, "to know what it is to be poor and to have plenty" (Phil. 4:12), for neither the one nor the other is outside the realm where the Father's will can be done.

Patently, prosperity makes the fulfillment of a vocation more difficult. Souls run the risk of being engulfed by riches which, at the least, fetter and restrict. St. Thomas held that

[7] *Vie de Notre-Seigneur Jésus-Christ,* II, p. 440.
[8] The same theme is developed in James 5:1-7.

"poverty is worthy of praise because by liberating man from earthly cares it allows him to concentrate more freely on things divine."[9] Considered in the light of the kingdom, real poverty is a privileged state because in it men are free. Let the rich man who believes that he owns his money take care lest his money own him. The demands of justice and charity are steadying forces and protect him from Christ's threat: "Woe to him who is not rich for God" (Luke 12:21). But Christ also speaks to those who have deep in their heart an ingrained hunger for riches — such is the meaning of His words about the treasure and the heart, the source of all desires (Luke 12:34).

> But those who seek to become rich fall into temptation and a snare and into many useless and harmful desires, which plunge men into destruction and damnation. For covetousness is the root of all evils, and some in their eagerness to get rich have strayed from the faith and have involved themselves in many troubles (1 Tim. 6:9-10).

One day Jesus refused to become involved when His followers were quarreling over an inheritance (Luke 12:13-15). His action was symbolic: "No matter how great are a man's possessions, they have no power to give him life." This thought seems no deeper than the criticism leveled against riches by Israel's sages: what are they worth in comparison with health, liberty and joy (Sir. 29:22; 30:14-16)? "The life is a greater thing than the food, and the body than the clothing" (Luke 12:23). But Jesus, referring to an Old Testament theme, goes further and recalls the kingdom which men must seek (Luke 12:31); He forces us to face the essential decision: "He who does not renounce all that he has cannot be my disciple" (Luke 14:33). Many passages quoted in the preceding pages are taken from St. Luke, the evangelist who best understood — perhaps due to the influence of his master St. Paul — how Christianity, in its basic option, was appreciated and welcomed by the poor of this world. No one has better avoided canonizing poverty in itself than he, no one has spoken of it with equal sympathy.

[9] *Contra Gentiles,* III, c. 133.

Poverty is also proposed as an apostolic ideal by Jesus.[10] His directives were preserved in "a handbook for missionaries" (Mark 6:8-11; Matthew 10:5-14; Luke 9:1-5), dear to Francis of Assisi and his first companions: "And he instructed them to take nothing for their journey, but a staff only — no wallet, no bread, no money in their girdle; but to wear sandals, and not to put on two tunics" (Mark 6:8-9). The "handbook" was meant for the Palestinian world where men's needs were few and strangers welcome. As the missionary horizon expanded, the "handbook" was enlarged; in the Matthew-Luke editions, gold and silver were specifically excluded. This fact gives us an insight into the meaning of apostolic poverty. It is a fidelity to the life of Jesus, to His joyously free poverty which was real but not deliberately ascetic. It is a fidelity that became creative in more complex civilizations. Imitation of Christ is not literal but inventive.

The life of St. Paul makes this clear. He handled large sums of money. There was a missionary budget to which the churches contributed (2 Cor. 11:8-9). Paul spent years collecting funds for the "saints" in Jerusalem. He was in a position to defray the losses Philemon had incurred at the hands of a fugitive slave (Phil. 1:19), to pay the sum required by the Temple authorities for the sacrifice offered by four Judaeo-Christians (Acts 21:23-24), to rent a house in Rome (Acts 28:30). In Caesarea about the year 62, the governor, hoping to receive some money, detained him in prison (Acts 24:26). Now in this land of olive trees where he traveled, "it is impossible to live, much less journey without money; in fact with money it is possible to practice poverty in the real sense of the word more sufferingly and more deliberately."[11] "To this very hour we hunger and thirst, and we are naked and buffeted, and have no fixed abode. And we toil, working with our own hands. We are reviled and we bless, we are persecuted and we bear with it" (1 Cor. 4:11-12; cf. 2 Cor. 11:9-27; Phil. 4:11-14). This poverty is more than

[10] A. George, "La pauvreté des apôtres," *Le Dieu des pauvres, Évangile*, 9, 1953, pp. 23-34.

[11] A. George, *op. cit.*, p. 29.

material deprivation. It includes sickness (2 Cor. 1:8-9), failure and persecution (2 Cor. 11:28). It is a communion with the poverty of Christ, who "became poor for your sakes, that by his poverty you might become rich" (2 Cor. 8:9).

Paul interprets Christ's life as a mystery of poverty, in which the apostle can share and to which he can give glory. We bear always "in our body the dying of Jesus, so that the life also of Jesus may be made manifest in our bodily frame" (2 Cor. 4:10). To meditate on the Cross is to realize that poverty is an integral part of the apostolate.

These three aspects of evangelical poverty introduce us to the major problem of this chapter — the beatitude of the poor. We have two versions of this beatitude at the beginning of the Sermon on the Mount. Luke writes: "Blessed are you poor, for yours is the kingdom of God" (6:20). Matthew says: "Blessed are the poor in spirit, for theirs is the kingdom of heaven" (5:3).

Certain truths can be established as basic. In the literal sense the context points to a common source, Aramaic Matthew, which was early translated into Greek (called Mg). Both versions preserve something of the original. Moreover, Jesus' audience cannot have consisted only of "the unfortunate, the lame, the disinherited who followed him into solitude."[12]

We know that the Twelve, at least, were listening to Him and that they were small landowners with homes and fishing boats of their own. Probably the crowd was a mixed one and, because they were in Galilee, the majority were *'am ha'areṣ*, poor relations of educated Israelites.[13] In those days no segment of the population corresponded to our suffering proletariat, a word we dislike to use because of all its inhuman connotations.

Jesus' audience must have included men whose limited possessions could never have come between them and God, others who did not always have enough to eat, some ordinary

[12] Régamey, *op. cit.*, p. 20.
[13] For the *'am ha'areṣ*, see footnote 6, chapter I, p. 18.

folk whom Jewish officials despised, the sick whom the Lord had recently cured (Matthew 4:24). All these people had only two things in common[14] — a secret longing for the kingdom and the name by which Jesus addressed them. The Aramaic word He used was either *'anya,* a synonym for *'ani* (Delitsch, Zahn, Allen), or *'anwan,* a synonym for *'anaw* (Joüon).[15] The semantic development of these two words made them identical in meaning.

To grasp the general meaning of the Beatitudes, they must be seen in the whole cadre of salvation-history. The men and women they honor are well known in the Old Testament. The Beatitudes "ratify and at the same time solemnly restate the principles that have always characterized Yahweh's supernatural government" (Matthew 5:17). This recapitulation of the divine promises in the Beatitudes when Jesus began to preach the coming of the kingdom is one of the first ways in which these promises were fulfilled. They are an affirmation of Yahweh's fidelity and of the continuity of religious life.[16] This was one of the "messianic works" according to the list drawn up in advance:

[14] The audience seems to have been homogeneous. Lagrange says, in reference to the four woes addressed to the rich (Luke 6:24-26), "Jesus was able to show by look or by a gesture that He was speaking to those at a distance, without losing sight of the needs of His immediate audience" — *Évangile selon saint Luc* (Paris: 1927), pp. 190-191.

[15] P. Joüon, S.J., *L'Évangile de Notre-Seigneur Jésus-Christ* (Paris: 1930), p. 20, suggests that the term used was *'anwana,* whose double meaning accounts for the two translations: "poor in spirit" and "meek." The same process may be observed in 11:29 (see p. 109). Lagrange (*L'Évangile selon saint Matthieu,* p. 83) also connects the beatitude of the poor and the meek.

[16] A. Lemonnyer, O.P., "Le messianisme des Béatitudes," *Revue des Sciences Philosophiques et Théologiques,* 1922, pp. 373-389. This article is basic. G. Feuillet, "La Béatitude de la pauvreté," *La Vie Spirituelle,* Dec. 1945, p. 512, #13, reached the same conclusions independently. J. Dupont (*Les Béatitudes: le problème littéraire, le message doctrinal,* Louvain, 1954) believes that the original form of the first Beatitude was "Blessed are the poor, for theirs is the kingdom of heaven." In these words Christ triumphantly proclaimed the messianic elevation of the *'anawim* and His presence was the guarantee that His words were fulfilled. The primitive meaning of the Beatitudes was, therefore, Christological. They correspond to the answer given to the Baptist's messengers (Luke 4:18-21). Matthew interpreted the Beatitudes as

> And in that day the deaf shall hear the words of the book; and out of darkness and obscurity the eyes of the blind shall see. And the meek (*'anawim*) shall increase their joy in Yahweh, and the poor men (*'ebyonim*) shall rejoice in the Holy One of Israel.[17]

We believe, therefore, that Matthew's statements, even though they may stress the spiritualization of themes of poverty, hunger and thirst, by way of added glosses,[18] are closer to the original than what Luke has to say. They are directly religious, while the Lucan Beatitudes evoke an immediately social context, and consequently the four "woes" that follow the Beatitudes are directed, without any possible spiritual transposition, to men who are actually rich, to the satisfied, to scoffers, to people of importance.[19] The author of the third Gospel seems to have given the Master's words a somewhat social meaning.[20]

Yet, let us make our own the most difficult hypothesis, that of L. Vaganay,[21] who believes Luke 6:20b ff is archaic in relation to Matthew 5:3ff. Does this mean that we must believe that Jesus "beatified a social class"? Has the Gospel any of the characteristics of a social manifesto? It canonizes no sociological state, nor places it in direct relation with the kingdom. A spiritual gift can be suitably received only in a

would a moralist, in the light of the basic theme of the Sermon on the Mount. Luke, conscious of the human reality of misery, explained *'anawim* in a social sense which represented only one aspect of the primitive Beatitude. In adding the "woes" that were not part of the source Mg, Luke clearly showed his interpretation.

17 Is. 29:18-19; cf. 26:19; 35:5-6; especially 61:1-3.

18 A. Descamps, *Les Justes et la Justice dans les évangiles et le christianisme primitif hormis la doctrine proprement paulinienne* (Louvain: 1950), pp. 164ff.

19 J. Bonsirven, *Théologie du Nouveau Testament* (Paris: 1951), pp. 135ff, 202.

20 This is, as we understand it, L. Cerfaux's position. Obviously it would hardly be critical to make Luke depend on Matthew. Yet even in Luke it is natural to think that a certain religious aura clings to the word "poor," even when used in an absolute sense. Lagrange remarked that "It is impossible to understand the word *ptochos* without taking into consideration the whole religious literature of the Jews where it is given a special meaning" (*Évangile selon saint Luc*, p. 187).

21 *La question synoptique* (Tournay: 1953), pp. 255, 291, 292, 305, 307.

spiritual situation. Only trusting faith can open man to God's grace. It is this openness to God that is called spiritual poverty. It is certain, and the Gospel says it plainly, that real poverty is a privileged path towards poverty of soul; it is the soil where the latter can more easily flourish; it is a state so precious that it is well worth the trouble of accepting it, even of seeking it, just as the mountain climber locates the best path for a difficult ascent. In this Beatitude Jesus does no more than repeat His *mašal* on the eye of the needle (Matthew 19:24). He recalls the condition and the prerequisites of a religious undertaking. This lesson deserves to be examined for its own sake. Herein is to be found the whole value of St. Matthew's words.

Osty gives this excellent translation: "Blessed are those who have the soul of a poor man," that is, "those who are conscious of their powerlessness to satisfy their aspirations for God's reign,"[22] who are "convinced of their spiritual indigence and of their need of redemption,"[23] those who lean entirely on God, never on themselves, "the indigent humble men who are so humble that they never stop begging for divine help,"[24] those whose disposition as "clients" prepares them to welcome the kingdom of God, the consolation of Israel (Luke 2:25) and the redemption of Jerusalem (Luke 2:38). In other words, they are the heirs of the mystical line of Israel whose summit we have found in the decisive moment of the Incarnation, when, through Mary, mankind opened itself wholly to the Gift from above.

We may say that this key word specifies a fundamental Christian attitude. It is linked with a central theme of Jesus' thought, the criticism of pharisaism.[25] The Pharisee is the man who believes that he is the artisan of his own salvation.

[22] Lagrange, *L 'Évangile de Jésus-Christ* (Paris: 1936), p. 142.

[23] Feuillet, *op. cit.*, p. 515.

[24] *Opus imperfectum in Mattheum,* P.L., 56, 680-681. The interpretation given in this sixth-century work is an improvement on that of St. Augustine: "Beati pauperes spiritu... quos sine ulla controversia humiles intelligimus" *(De sancta virginitate,* 32, P.L., 40, 413).

[25] Walther Sattler has seen this clearly in *Die 'Anawim im Zeitalter Jesu Christi* (Tübingen: 1927).

He is convinced that his justice is the result of some human technique. Permeated by Jewish voluntarism, he structures his own sanctity and prepares the ears of corn that the divine Harvester need only gather. He believes himself to be just (Luke 18:9), he speaks of *his* justice (Phil. 3:9), he never transgresses God's commands (Luke 15:29). Yet his error is capital. God never finds in him the renunciation, the surrender, the opening through which grace can enter. In a paradoxical fashion Jesus contrasts him with the publican. After reading the parable in which the two religious types are opposed, members of study-groups sometimes speak of the "rich Pharisee" and the "poor publican." Socially the adjectives should be reversed. But money alone does not make a man rich; the Pharisee felt that he was rich in *his* merits, *his* perseverance. Enclosing himself in his own self-sufficiency, he cut himself off from the Source. The publican had the soul of a "poor" man and was open to the Source.[26]

It is remarkable that Therese of the Child Jesus discovered the way of spiritual childhood in the Pauline criticism of Pharisaism. This Gospel theme is also in harmony with the first Beatitude. We must open ourselves to the energies of the kingdom, just like the little children whom Jesus loved. "Whoever does not accept the kingdom of God as a little child will not enter into it" (Mark 10:15).

Two passages proper to St. Matthew accord perfectly with the first Beatitude as he has formulated it. The reference in each instance is to Jesus Himself. According to Vaganay, Matthew 11:28-30 comes from a source complementary to the Greek version of Matthew; this fragment has been used but was not influenced by Luke. Opposing His way of teaching to rabbinic methods, Jesus offers His own legislation as set down in the Sermon on the Mount to those who were weighed down by the burden of Pharisaic observances: "Learn of me, for I am meek and humble of heart *(praüs kai tapeinos te kardia)*." The original source may have merely contained the words, "I am *'anaw*" (Aramaic, *'anwana)*,[27] and the por-

[26] Cf. Apoc. 3:17-18.
[27] Cf. p. 106, footnote 15.

trait may have been made more explicit through the use of two Greek words expressing the notes of humility and condescension. Expressed was Christ's obedient humility before His Father, in His role as Messiah, and His fraternal humility before men, full of understanding, modesty and meekness (Matthew 12:19-20). Christian tradition did not forget this portrait; Paul linked humility and meekness *(tapeinophrosyne* and *praütes* in Col. 3:12; Eph. 4:2). He probably coined the first term and slanted it towards charity. St. Peter made use of the term to situate the life of the Christian in God's presence.

The statement about Jesus' messianic entry into Jerusalem (Matthew 21:5) recalls the prophecy of Zechariah (9:9) where the Messiah is called *'ani.*[28] This citation is found only in the first Gospel and is probably borrowed from a collection of texts. It is another example of Matthew's attraction for terms that describe Jesus' humble soul and seems to preserve a reflection of the Servant of Yahweh prophecy. A rapprochement has been proposed with the messianic figure of Solomon's Psalm 17: "He places not his trust in horse, horseman or bow; he does not muster an army for his defense on the day of battle. The Lord is his king and his hope: he is powerful because he trusts in God."

Yet we know well that the title *'ani-'anaw* attributed to Moses and David does not evoke in all its tragic dimensions this mystery of poverty-humility in which Christ entered to save us. The Bethlehem stable, dear to Father Chevrier, the laborious obscurity of Nazareth, dear to Father de Foucauld, the choice of a suffering messianism in the desert of Judah, the failure in Galilee and Jerusalem and lastly the Cross — were these not the stages of a *tapeinosis* more profound than that hymned in advance by the Second-Isaiah? To sum up all this, Paul made use of the old vocabulary of poverty:

> ...appearing in the form of man he humbled himself *(etapeinose)*, becoming obedient to death, even to death on a cross (Phil. 2: 7-8).

[28] Cf. p. 90.

Conclusion

The subject we have attempted in these pages is, from a biblical point of view, highly complex.[1] Its aspects are multiple, its "route" not always easily identified, its vocabulary at times ambiguous. Because a "Bible man" is the real man whom God is teaching how "to walk" (Hosea 11:1), it may be said that each one of us recognizes himself in these sons of Abraham whose faults, temptations and sins are known to God, and whose aspirations, conversions and heroisms are directed by Him. Their problems continue to be our problems, their experiences correspond to our experiences. That is why the subject does not find us indifferent; our heart is involved in spite of ourselves,[2] because divine revelation is here focused on those things that are fundamental in man.

Let us recall what these fundamentals are. The whole Bible from Amos to St. James and from Deuteronomy to Jesus considers poverty (and the word has an extension greater than the simple privation of money) as an extreme state disturbing to our conscience. The correctives proposed in the inspired pages are dated. No claim is made that their repetition and slavish imitation will suffice until the end of time. However,

[1] This is the impression found in "Le temps du pauvre," *Jeunesse de l'Église*, 9 (1948), where attempts to trace many "routes" are found. Note this comment made by one of these authors: There is no consciousness of poverty unless there is conscious poverty.

[2] The violence, in some ways unjustified, of such a reaction is found in J. Massin, *Le festin chez Lévi* (Paris: 1952).

in these recommendations, there is more than realism. In spite of a certain tendency (fairly localized, in our opinion) to equate the poor man and the sinner, there is the observation that the poor become religious more easily than the rich, because they are less likely to be self-sufficient and consequently closer to God. This is notably true of those "little ones" so dear to biblical authors, the poor who are somewhere in between opulence and indigence. This is a theme of Proudhon clearly enunciated in the Old Testament. In any case, the critique of riches, made from a religious point of view, never ceased from the prophets to Jesus. It is He who, having chosen poverty as a means of the redemption, consecrated it as a value. Henceforth, each poor man, with his own special kind of poverty, is a reminder and, as it were, a sacrament of the great Poor Man proclaimed by the Second-Isaiah.

With Zephaniah, the vocabulary of poverty underwent a spiritual transformation and served to denote man before God in the religious attitude of client. We have tried to give a concrete description of this mystical lineage of Israel, so anonymously eloquent in the psalter, but which also includes famous names like Jeremiah, the author of the book of Job, and above all Mary, the lowly maid who at the threshold of the New Covenant recapitulates all the spiritual depths of the Old. Poverty thus understood is a modality of faith. It is abandoned, trusting and joyous, closely akin to humility. It shows itself in an attitude of religious waiting. The Beatitude of the poor in Matthew's Gospel is focused on this fundamental disposition, and its various aspects are continued in the critique of pharisaism so central in the Gospel, as well as in the parable of the children, which is, as it were, the antithesis of this critique.

These two poverties, effective poverty and spiritual poverty, are concretely connected. Historically, the second is rooted in the first. As a matter of fact, to enable spiritual poverty to flourish, the Essenians bound themselves by a vow of poverty. And Christ confirmed what tradition had discovered. None of these biblical lessons were nor should be lost. Without pretending to extract from the Bible an economic treatise, we have no right to forget the social results of its religious principles. Jesus did not claim to organize the world, but He was actually speaking to men of flesh and blood and we know where His preferences led.[3]

Evangelical poverty, as He practiced it, continues in the Church as an unmistakably clear sign of an understanding of His spirit. The saint who most closely resembled Him is, perhaps, the Poverello of Assisi. Franciscan poverty is at once liberation, joy, brotherhood and union with Jesus.[4] Charles de Foucauld and Père Chevrier have given it new dimensions and it is treasured as a heritage by their apostolic families.[5]

According to Régamey, evangelical poverty in its final profundity is a "radical renunciation," a total humility and consequently a limitless trust in God. It is this basic disposition that the Bible has described in some of its best pages. It is this insight that is the greatness of the mystical descendants of Israel. Mary's life shows us all its beauty, Jesus' life all its value, for it was He, the *'anaw*, who declared that the poor of heart are blessed. This theme was handed down from generation to generation as the very secret of sanctity.

In the majestic *Veni Creator* the Church asks us to sing to the Holy Spirit, "*Veni, pater pauperum* — Come, Father of the poor." Masters of the spiritual life repeat with Bérulle: "Our attitude in prayer should be that of the truly poor." This was surely the basic message entrusted to the young saint of Lisieux for our generation so desirous of going back to the sources. It is a joy to close this study with some notes she has left us:

"Sanctity does not consist of this or that practice but of a disposition of heart that places us, humble and little, in God's arms, conscious of our weakness and confident to the point of boldness in His paternal goodness. . . . What makes

[3] See H. Jonte, *Idées de Jésus sur la pauvreté et la richesse* (Paris: 1900).

[4] Régamey, *op. cit.*, pp. 78-81.

[5] For Charles de Foucauld, see Voillaume, *Seeds of the Desert* (London: 1955). For Père Chevrier, see Ancel, *La pauvreté du prêtre d'après la vie et les écrits du Vénérable Antoine Chevrier* (Lyons: 1939).

my soul pleasing (to the good God) is the way I love my littleness and my poverty, and the way I trust blindly in His mercy....

> *"Fear not — the more you are poor, the more Jesus will love you."*[6]

[6] See A. Combes, *The Spirituality of St. Thérèse* (New York: 1949). On p. 134, after recalling the importance of Romans 4:4-6 in Thérèse's spirituality, the author adds this commentary which says everything: "Spiritual infancy involves an understanding of the gratuitous nature of our redemption and a desire to receive it as a free gift of God."

Texts

ISAIAN DIATRIBE AGAINST PRIDE[1]

(Your Face, Yahweh, is turned against Israel)

6. For you have cast off your people, the house of Jacob: because they are filled as in times past, and have had soothsayers as the Philistines, and have adhered to strange children.
7. Their land is filled with silver and gold: and there is no end of their treasures.
8. And their land is filled with horses: and their chariots are innumerable. Their land also is full of idols: they have adored the work of their own hands, which their own fingers have made.
9. And man has bowed himself down: and man has been debased. Therefore forgive them not.
11. The lofty eyes of man are humbled, and the haughtiness of men shall be made to stoop: and Yahweh alone shall be exalted in that day.
12. Because the day of Yahweh of hosts shall be upon every

[1] Is. 2:6-22. In chapter two mention was made of the importance of Isaiah, on whom Zephaniah based his spiritual synthesis. The passage cited above is celebrated. The additions made to it attest an intensive reading in Israel. We are able to distinguish three glosses: anti-idolatry verses (vv. 18, 20-21); moralizing conclusion (v. 22, which is missing in the Septuagint); lastly vv. 9c-10, affected by v. 19. The restored first line is purely conjectural.

one that is proud and highminded, and upon every one that is arrogant: and he shall be humbled.

13. And upon all the tall and lofty cedars of Libanus, and upon all the oaks of Bashan.
14. And upon all the high mountains, and upon all the elevated hills.
15. And upon every high tower, and every fenced wall.
16. And upon all the ships of Tarshish, and upon all that is fair to behold.
17. And the loftiness of men shall be bowed down: and the haughtiness of men shall be humbled. And Yahweh alone shall be exalted in that day.
19. And they shall go into the holes of rocks and into the caves of the earth, from the face of the fear of Yahweh and from the glory of his majesty, when he shall rise up to strike the earth.

ST. AUGUSTINE: COMMENTARY ON THE FIRST BEATITUDE[2]

Who are the poor in spirit? The humble, men trembling at God's words, confessing their sins, relying neither on their own merits, nor on their own righteousness. Who are the poor in spirit? They who when they do anything good praise God, when anything evil accuse themselves. "Upon whom shall rest my Spirit," said the prophet, "but upon the humble man and peaceful and trembling at My words" (Is. 66:2). Now Asaph has understood, he no longer cleaves to the earth, he no longer insists on the earthly promises of the Old Testament; he has become Your beggar, he has become Your poor one; he thirsts for Your rivers, his own have dried up. Because he has changed in this way, let not his hopes be frustrated; he has searched for You during the night, stretching out his hand to You; let him not be disappointed (Ps. 76:3). Confessing their sins, they will glorify Your name: not those who are puffed up because of their temporal goods, not those who are proud and elated because

[2] See pp. 34, 108.

of their own righteousness. Who then? "The poor and the needy will glorify Your name" (Commentary on Psalm 73).

ST. BASIL: RICH AND POOR[3]

What answer will you give to the (sovereign) Judge, you who cover the walls and do not clothe those who resemble you? You who find ornaments for your horses and do not even consider the distress of your brother? You who allow your wheat to rot and do not feed the hungry? You who hide your gold and do not come to the aid of the oppressed?

Whom have I harmed, you reply, in keeping what is mine? Tell me, does what I possess belong to you?

From whom did you receive it, to enjoy it during your life? You are like a man who buys a ticket for a seat in a theater, refuses to allow any one else to enter and acts as if he owned what is meant to be used by all. This is what rich men do. Because they are the first to enjoy a good common to all, they think they have a right to appropriate it. If each one contented himself with the strictly necessary and gave all the rest to the needy, there would be neither rich nor poor. Did you not come naked from your mother's womb? Will you not return naked to the earth? As for your present possessions, from whom have you received them?

If you answer that they are yours by chance, you are impious and refuse to acknowledge your Creator and repay your benefactor with thanks. If you agree that they come from God, tell me why you have received them. Is He so unjust as to divide the necessities of life unequally among men? Why should you have more than you need and another man not enough? Is it not so that you may one day receive the reward of your good and faithful stewardship, while he will be given a crown for his patience? But you who hold on to all your possessions with abysmal avarice, think you harm no one, while you are depriving so many others like yourself.

[3] *Hom.* VII, 4; *Hom.* VI, 7. St. Basil has recaptured something of the verve of the prophets and the vehemence of their charity.

PRAYER OF ST. FRANCIS OF ASSISI TO OBTAIN THE GRACE OF POVERTY[4]

(Composed by Ubertino in 1305 and attributed to St. Francis. This prayer inspired Dante, *Paradiso*, XI, 64-66, 70-72).

O my most sweet Lord Jesus Christ, have pity on me and on my Lady Poverty, for I burn with love of her, and without her I cannot rest. O my Lord, who did cause me to be enamoured of her, You know that she is sitting in sadness, rejected by all; "the mistress of nations is become as a widow," vile and contemptible; the queen of all virtues, seated on a dunghill, complains that all her friends have despised her, and are become her enemies; they have proved themselves deceivers, and not spouses.

Behold, O Lord Jesus, how truly Poverty is the queen of all the virtues; for, leaving the abode of angels, You did come down to earth that You might espouse her to Yourself with constant love, and produce from her, in her, and by her, the children of all perfection. . . . At Your birth she received You in a manger and a stable; and during Your life she so stripped You of all things that she would not even allow You a stone whereon to rest Your head.

As a most faithful consort she accompanied You when You did go forth to fight for our redemption; and in the conflict of Your passion she alone stood by as Your armor-bearer. When Your disciples fled, and denied Your name, she did not leave You, but, with the whole band of her princes, she fearlessly adhered to You.

On account of the height of Your Cross, even Your Mother (who devotedly loved You and shared so deeply in the bitterness of Your passion) could not reach You; but Your Lady Poverty, with companion Want, embraced You more closely than ever, and was more firmly united to You in Your sufferings. Therefore, she would not allow Your Cross to be smoothed or in any way polished; the very nails were (as it is believed) too few in number, not sharpened nor ground; but she provided only three — blunt, thick, and rough — in order to increase Your torments.

[4] Frederick Ozanam, *The Franciscan Poets*, pp. 60-62.

And when You were consumed with thirst, she, Your faithful spouse, was there, and did not allow You to have even a drop of water; but by means of the impious executioners she prepared for You a draught so bitter that You could only taste, not drink it. In the strong embrace of this Your spouse, You did breathe forth Your soul. Nor did she forsake You at Your burial, but she took care that You should have neither sepulcher, nor ointments, nor winding-cloths, except what were lent You by others.

Thus Your holy spouse was not absent from Your resurrection, for rising gloriously in her embrace You did leave in the sepulcher all these borrowed things. You did bear her with You to heaven, leaving all that is in the world. And now You have given to Your Lady Poverty the seal of Your kingdom, that she may sign the elect who walk in the way of perfection. Oh, who would not love the Lady Poverty above all! I beseech You to grant me this privilege: I beg to be enriched with this much-desired treasure.

O most poor Jesus, I ask this favor for myself and my children for ever, that for love of You they may never possess anything of their own, that they may use the goods of others sparingly, and that they may suffer Poverty as long as they live in this miserable world.

ST. JOHN OF THE CROSS: TO ESTABLISH THE SOUL IN SPIRITUAL POVERTY[5]

Let [spiritual directors] strive to disencumber the soul and to set it in a state of rest, in such a way that it will not be bound to any one kind of knowledge, whether above or below, or to any covetousness of sweetness or pleasure, nor to any other apprehension, but that it will be empty in pure negation with respect to every creature and will be established in poverty of spirit. It is this that the soul must do as far as in it lies, as the Son of God counsels, saying: "Everyone of you who does not renounce all that he possesses cannot be my disciple" (Luke 14:33). This is to be understood not only of the renunciation of all temporal things with the will,

[5] *The Living Flame of Love*, 3,3.

but also of the surrender of spiritual things, in which consists poverty of spirit wherein the Son of God places blessedness (Matthew 5:3; Luke 6:20).

When the soul in this way frees itself of all things and succeeds in emptying itself and surrendering them — which we have said is the part that the soul can play — it is impossible, if the soul does all that it can, that God should fail to perform His own part by communicating Himself to the soul, at least secretly and silently. It is more impossible than that the sun should fail to shine in a serene and unclouded sky; for as the sun when it rises in the morning will enter your house if you open the shutter, even so will God, who sleeps not in guarding Israel, much less slumbers (Ps. 120:4), enter the soul that is empty and fill it with divine blessings.

THE PRAYER OF POVERTY ACCORDING TO BÉRULLE[6]

When we are at prayer we should think and act as do the poor. When they knock at a door they wait patiently until something is brought to them; then, avoiding anything like importunity, they knock again. This is what the soul does who knows its own poverty and need and who also sees that it deserves only hell for its offenses. This soul, I say, humbles and abases itself before the majesty of God and seeks in all kinds of ways to soften His anger and draw to itself His mercy, by sometimes knocking meekly at heaven's gate by acts of humility and compunction, acts of knowledge of its own nothingness and God's splendor; by sometimes patiently waiting until it please God to come to its rescue and relieve its wretchedness.

MONSIEUR OLIER'S OPPOSITION TO A PROPRIETARY SPIRIT[7]

The spirit of Christianity requires that Christians be transplanted and moved from the branch of Adam to the Word Incarnate, so that drawing their life and strength from

[6] Rule of the Congregation of the Oratory. M. Olier also recommends that the soul remain in God's presence "like a poor beggar."

[7] *Vie et vertus chrétiennes*, ch. XI, 8. *Letters* I, p. 588.

Him, they will no longer live with their own life but will act in Him alone.

Therefore, we should hold nothing in as much horror as proprietorship that deprives us of the fullness of the Word, of His life, of His action, and that keeps us in this admirable body as useless members incapable of any true or solid good; but where, on the contrary, with self-abnegation followed by establishment in Jesus Christ, one is all and can do all in God.

This explains why our Lord in His gospel made abnegation the first step that must be taken in Christian life! If anyone wants to come after Me, let him renounce himself because proprietorship and fullness of self block the entrance of Jesus Christ and the fullness of His divine life and are an unending source of all evils and all sins. . . . When I speak to you of property, I do not mean that gross form of property consisting of exterior things. I am referring to every kind of inward and hidden property, as well as property of the mind, the reason, the judgment, the will, for these are the chief obstacles to the Spirit and His life; He makes His home in these secret depths and it should be pure, holy, empty of every trace of self, so that the Spirit may fill all.

BOSSUET'S APOSTROPHE TO THE RICH[8]

I say to you, O rich men of this age, that you do wrong to treat the poor with such unmerited disdain, so that you will know, if we wish to go to the root of the matter, that we will find that they have no less right than you to the goods you possess. Nature, or to speak in a more Christian manner, God, the common Father of men, has given from the beginning an equal right to all His children over all the things they need to maintain life. No one of us can boast that we are better off by nature, but the insatiable desire of increasing our possessions did not allow this beautiful fraternity to last long in this world. This led to division and to property and is responsible for all the quarrels and all the lawsuits. This

[8] Taken from Bossuet's "Panegyric on St. Francis of Assisi." Here, rather than in his "Sermon on the eminent dignity of the poor in the Church," are to be found his best pages on poverty.

explains the words "mine" and "thine" that St. John Chrysostom says are so cold. This accounts for the many different social levels: some live with an abundance of all things, others languish in extreme want. This is why several of the holy Fathers, noting both the origin of things and nature's general liberality towards all men, unhesitatingly declared that to refuse to give of our superfluity to the poor is to deprive them of what is rightfully theirs.

THE SONG OF THE PARIAH, THE BARBER[9]

The Spirit of Blessing has passed before my house,
 The house that belongs to me, the barber!
I ran, He turned and waited for me,
 Me, the barber!
I said: "May I speak to You, O Lord?"
 And He said: "Yes."
And I said: "May I follow You?"
 And He said: "Yes."
 Even *me,* the barber!
And I said: "May I stay near You, O Lord?"
 And He said: "You may."
 Even *me,* the poor barber!

PRAYERS OF THE POOR OF ANCIENT EGYPT[10]

1. You are Amon, the Lord of the silent ones (gr)
  who comes to the cry of the poor (nmḥw).
 I call upon you in my distress,
  and you come to deliver me.

[9] This piece of ancient Buddhist literature was given to me by P. Dieux of the Oratory. It is cited by L. Adams Beck, *A la découverte du Yoga* (Paris: 1938), p. 305.

[10] Barucq, "Péché et innocence dans les psaumes bibliques et les textes religieux de l'Égypte du Nouvel Empire," *Études de critique et d'histoire religieuse* (Lyons: 1948), pp. 111-137, has studied some texts coming from the people that are full of the religion of the heart. (1) Stele of Neb-Rê, under Ramses II, c. 1250 (tr. Drioton). The complete text is found in P. Gilbert, *La poésie égyptienne* (Brussels: 1949), pp. 80-82. (2) Papyrus Anastasi II, c. 1200 (tr. Barucq). (3) Acclamation addressed to a dead man, on the base of his statue, perhaps fifteenth century (tr. Barucq).

You give life to the wretched,
you deliver me when I am a captive.
2. Amon, lend an ear to one
who stands alone before the tribunal!
He is poor (nmḥw),
while the other one is rich.
The court crushes him.
"Give money for the assessors!"
"Give cloth for the employees!"
Amon is going to turn into a Vizier
so that he can make the poor (nmḥw) triumph.
Behold the poor (nmḥw) will be justified
and the wretched (nmḥw) will surpass the rich...
I do not place my hope in any man's strength...
It is my Lord who will be my defender.
I know the strength that has won for him the name
"The defender with the powerful arm."
3. Twice happy is he who rests blessedly on Amon's arm,
he who cares for the silent (gr)
who helps the poor (nmḥw)
and gives life to those he loves.

FATHER CHEVRIER'S ELEGY TO A POOR PRIEST[11]

How beautiful is this man of God whose feet scarcely touch the earth! *Quam pulchri pedes evangelizantium pacem, evangelizantium bona!* What freedom and what power the holy and beautiful poverty of Jesus Christ gives the priest! What strength he wins to fight against the vices of the world! What an example he is to the world, the world that works only for money, that thinks only of money, that lives only for money! And beside this material, sensual world is the wholly spiritual man who does not live for the world and who despises money and temporal goods... who gives to anyone who asks, who is satisfied with the strictly necessary,

[11] This extract of "The true disciple of Our Lord Jesus Christ" is a translation of Msgr. Ancel's text: *Essai sur la spiritualité du P. Chevrier*, pp. 20-21.

who asks nothing of anyone, who works for God alone... who abandons himself to the hands of divine Providence.

How fine, how great, how admirable is this man! And how the world should turn on seeing him and admire in him the power of faith, of love, of trust in God. Where are these men? They will do wonderful things, says Wisdom.

O Poverty, how beautiful you are! Jesus Christ, my Master, found you so beautiful that He wished to espouse you when He came down from heaven, He wished to make you the companion of His whole life, and He wished to die with you on the cross.

Give me, O my Master, this beautiful Poverty. Grant that I may seek her with care, that I may possess her with faith, that I may embrace her with love, that I may make her the companion of my whole life, just like St. Francis, my Father, the truly poor man of Jesus Christ, and that I may die with her on a piece of wood, like my Master.

THE GATE OF THE KINGDOM[12]

To be poor is not interesting; all poor people agree about this.

It is interesting to possess the kingdom of heaven, but only the poor possess it.

Nor should we think that our joy consists in spending our days emptying our hands, our heads, our hearts.

It is our joy to spend our days making room in our hands, our heads, our hearts, for the kingdom of heaven that passes.

Because it is unheard to know He is near, to know God is so near us, it is prodigious to know His love possible to such a degree in us and on us.

And not to open this door to Him, the unique and simple door of poverty of spirit.

Free yourself from self-interest, for it is a luxury to take so much care of yourself: while old age will speak to you of birth, and death of resurrection;

time will seem like a little fold on the greatness of

[12] Madeleine Delbrel, in *Études carmélitaines*, 1947, pp. 185-187.

eternity; you will judge all things according to their eternal values.

If you love the kingdom of heaven with true love, you will rejoice because your intelligence is at a loss before things divine and you will try to believe better.

If your prayer is stripped of tender emotions, you will know that God does not reach you through your feelings.

If you are without great courage, you will rejoice that you are ready for hope.

If you find that people bore you and that your heart is breaking, you will be happy that you possess within you charity that cannot be perceived.

When you are stripped of all things, you will no longer be able to see the world as anything more than a pillaged house,

yourself as but indigence without any façade,

think of those shadowed eyes open in the center of your soul, fixed on things ineffable,

because the kingdom of heaven is within you.

EVANGELICAL POVERTY[13]

The poverty of Jesus is a life-giving mystery. The further we penetrate into that mystery, the better we shall see how utterly one the gospel life is. It is from the love of Him who is the infinitely simple, of Him who is sovereign poverty incarnate, that poverty heads, and its natural flow is towards love of the little and the wretched; humble itself, it cannot live with hardness or pride.

Proud poverty, hard poverty is a dead thing that estranges us from Jesus. True poverty is at the same time one of the roads to inner silence and contemplative prayer, when founded on self-dispossession and the liberty of the soul with regard to all the created. True, living poverty is gentle, tender towards suffering, glad and open-hearted, and always ready to give or lend. It is likewise at peace and without fear; for it is before all else childlike self-abandon in the hands of the God who is Love, of the God who is a Father.

[13] R. Voillaume, *Seeds of the Desert* (London: 1955), pp. 276-277. No commentary on the biblical *'anawah* could be more beautiful!

Liturgical Press

BIBLE publications

BIBLE AND LITURGY SUNDAY BULLETIN

A parish, Sunday bulletin (8½ x 12½), blank on reverse side for parish announcements; text and art edited to implement the new trends in emphasizing Sacred Scripture and liturgical renewal.

SCRIPTURE SERVICES

20 Bible themes arranged and edited for immediate use in parishes, chapels, convents; parts distributed among participants are clearly indicated.

LEARNING TO READ THE BIBLE

18 pedagogical tips to make daily Bible reading a fascinating religious experience; an initiation guide for beginners.

THE PARISH BIBLE-CLASS

A detailed exposition of the method on how to conduct study sessions on the Sacred Scriptures on the parish level. Eminently practical throughout.

CHILDREN'S BIBLE

Tells the Scripture story from creation to our Lord's Second Coming in simple and dignified narrative — with 84 illustrations in color. Already widely used in the early grades.

CHILDREN'S BIBLE — A SPOKEN RECORD

A 33⅓ recording of the complete text of the CHILDREN'S BIBLE.

THE PSALMS ARE OUR PRAYERS

A companion booklet to *The Poor of Yahweh* leading us not only to appreciate the psalms in a literary way but also to pray them.

GOD'S WORD AND WORK — The Message of the Old Testament Historical Books

Used as an *introduction* to the Old Testament historical books on a secondary level. A fine review of needed background to understand the spiritual message of the books treated.

DAILY BIBLE READING WITH THE CHURCH

A reading program by which the entire Bible is covered in a two-year period.

PSALMS FOR BEGINNERS

A selection of 60 psalms with titles, strophe headings, and brief introductions. Priced in the give-away bracket.

MARY, QUEEN OF THE POOR

Father Barnabas Ahern here provides us with an approach to Marian thinking that is solidly Biblical and universally inspiring.

THE MEN AND THE MESSAGE OF THE OLD TESTAMENT

A comprehensive, up-to-date coverage of material required for an intelligent reading of all the books from Genesis to 2 Machabees. 604 pages. Maps.

GREEK, LATIN, ENGLISH STUDENTS' NEW TESTAMENT WORKBOOK

The text of Nestle's New Testament, with English Confraternity version, on each page — leaving ¼ of each page blank for personal notes.

ILLUSTRATED NEW TESTAMENT

Complete text; illustrated by over 500 photos of exceptional historical and archeological value. 8½ x 11; 256 pages.

NEW TESTAMENT READING GUIDE

A series of 14 booklets covering the whole New Testament. Each booklet contains (a) complete text of New Testament book treated; (b) introduction discussing author, time, place of composition, purpose, content; (c) a full commentary on the text, verse by verse; (d) review aids and discussion topics.

Titles and authors:

INTRODUCTION TO THE NEW TESTAMENT
Roderick A. F. MacKenzie, S.J.

GOSPEL OF ST. MARK
Gerard S. Sloyan

GOSPEL OF ST. LUKE
Carroll Stuhlmueller, C.P.

GOSPEL OF ST. MATTHEW
David M. Stanley, S.J.

ACTS OF THE APOSTLES
Neal M. Flanagan, O.S.M.

INTRODUCTION TO THE PAULINE LETTERS —
1 — 2 THESSALONIANS
Bruce Vawter, C.M.

GALATIANS — ROMANS
Barnabas M. Ahern, C.P.

1 — 2 CORINTHIANS
Claude J. Peifer, O.S.B.

CAPTIVITY LETTERS
Kathryn Sullivan, R.S.C.J.

PASTORAL LETTERS
Robert T. Siebeneck, C.PP.S.

HEBREWS
John F. McConnell, M.M.

JAMES, JUDE, PETER
Eugene H. Maly

GOSPEL OF ST. JOHN AND THE JOHANNINE EPISTLES
Raymond E. Brown, S.S.

THE APOCALYPSE
William G. Heidt, O.S.B.